Reading *Cultivating F_____e
and stirring me in the _____, __1e
stories of answered prayer, and each devotional has left me hungry for more!
Beautifully written, heart-warming, encouraging, and powerful!

—Jean Melnick
Mission Director, Samaritan Foundation
Dominican Republic

The scriptures make a clear statement of the power of testimony, which is
on full display in Ruth Teakle's devotional, *Cultivating Faith*, through her own
stories and those of fellow followers of Jesus. This skilled author will take
you into the vivid events of the Bible. In every testimony, faith is in action!
Your faith will be activated too, so be prepared—there just might be a few
tears of marvel and awe at the creative, supernatural ways of God!

—Rev. Peggy I. Kennedy
Two Silver Trumpets Ministry
Speaker, Author of *A is for Apple*, *Chosen*, and *Hear the Sound*.

Without faith it's impossible to please God. We are justified by faith. Faith
comes by hearing, and hearing by the Word of God. These devotionals centre
our attention on a critical attribute of our Christian lives. They are focused,
challenging, and inspirational. They will penetrate your heart and soul and
strengthen your personal faith journey.

—Allan Gallant
Co-Founder and Executive Director, Agora Network Ministries

Ruth's biblical devotional thoughts are woven together with powerful personal
testimonies. Issues like fear, weariness, and a need for hope are just some of
the topics addressed. Each daily reading will refresh your spirit and renew your
faith. If you're looking for something both relevant and practical in dealing
with the everyday stuff of life we all face, I highly recommend *Cultivating Faith*.

—Paul Willoughby
Former Producer/Host of *Nite Lite Live*
Author of *Don't Waste Your Pain*

Cultivating Faith

Cultivating Faith

A 30 Day Devotional Journey

Ruth Teakle
& a Company of Friends

CULTIVATING FAITH
Copyright © 2021 by Ruth Teakle

Printed in Canada

Print ISBN: 978-1-4866-2204-7
eBook ISBN: 978-1-4866-2205-4

Word Alive Press
119 De Baets Street, Winnipeg, MB R2J 3R9
www.wordalivepress.ca

MIX
Paper from
responsible sources
FSC® C103567

WORD ALIVE
— P R E S S —

Cataloguing in Publication may be obtained through Library and Archives Canada

Contents

Getting Started

> *"But the fruit produced by the Holy Spirit within you is divine love in all its varied expressions: joy that overflows, peace that subdues, patience that endures, kindness in action, a life full of virtue,* faith that prevails, *gentleness of heart, and strength of spirit . . . they are meant to be limitless."*
>
> —Galatians 5:22–23b, TPT (emphasis added)

The opening verses of Hebrews 11, that familiar chapter on faith, say:

> *Now faith is the substance of things hoped for, the evidence of things not seen. For by it the elders obtained a good testimony. By faith we understand that the worlds were framed by the word of God, so that the things which are seen were not made of things which are visible.*
>
> —Hebrews 11:1–3, NKJV

This passage isn't simply a definition of faith but more a summary of what faith does. Faith is the substance that securely binds us as believers to the reality of what we don't yet see but confidently expect. Through trust in God, we experience His power in our lives and confirm His reality. Having faith means living life with our eyes turned Heavenward, knowing and believing God's promises to be true. As our eyes of faith are opened, we begin to see the greatness of God's power available on our behalf. While the world says "Seeing is believing," in God's Kingdom, *believing* always precedes *seeing.*

Our initial relationship with God is by faith, a faith that brings us into salvation in Christ. Our hope for eternal life is also by faith. Faith enables us to venture courageously into an unseen future, supported by the Word of God. Our faith strengthens us to endure through difficult times and allows us to "carry" others to God when they're too weak or broken to do so themselves. Obedient faith leads us to see God's promises fulfilled in our lives.

Everything we do is a matter of faith, and for faith to increase, it must be cultivated. Jesus assures us in Matthew that even "little faith" (the size of a grain of mustard seed) can accomplish great things for the Kingdom. The Holy Spirit is at work in us expressing Divine love through *a faith that prevails.* On the other hand, lacking faith, or partnering with doubt, can hold back the fulness of all God wants to accomplish through us, and it can actually be offensive to God.

This devotional will stir your faith and encourage you to live it loudly! Jesus is who He says He is. God's promises are true: we are meant to live in His power and liberty, with our eyes fixed on Him. In these pages, you'll discover testimonies of enduring faith, saving faith, tested faith, amazing faith, and "little faith." Each story is unique, heartfelt, and vulnerable. As well, you will become reacquainted with some familiar Bible personalities from the "hall of faith," and a few "uncommon" heroes of faith who have something significant to teach us.

Take time to pause with the scriptures that begin each day's reading and let the Word of God speak to you. Pray the prayers at the end of each devotional, adding your own thoughts, laments, or requests. My prayer for you is Ephesians 3:16–17:

> *. . . that he would unveil within you the unlimited riches of his glory and favor until supernatural strength floods your innermost being with his divine might and explosive power. Then,* by constantly using your faith, *the life of Christ will be released deep inside you, and the resting place of his love will become the very source and root of your life.* (TPT, emphasis added)

Desperate Faith

Day One

"*He said to her, 'Daughter, your faith has healed you. Go in peace and be freed from your suffering.'*"

—Mark 5:34

An old but familiar statement relates that "Desperate times call for desperate measures." In the scripture passages related to our selected verse (Matthew 9:18–26; Mark 5:21–43; Luke 8:40–56), we read the story of a woman whose faith was exercised to the full in desperation, a woman who had been bleeding for twelve demoralizing years. With her health gone, and now the bulk of her wealth spent on doctors, she was at the end of her rope. She had tried her best, at great cost, but she wasn't willing to give up!

Demonstrating great courage, she was willing to interrupt Jesus as He hurried to fulfil a priority mission—to restore to life the daughter of Jairus. As she elbowed her way through the crowd, she risked rejection, public humiliation, and possible stoning. Her faith propelled her forward as she held on to the certainty of what Jesus would do for her if she could just reach Him! She thought, "*If I just touch his clothes, I will be healed*" (Mark 5:28b). What a powerful conviction for a woman who had spent twelve years fighting what appeared to be a losing battle. She realized it would be safest to be inconspicuous, blend in with the crowd, coming just close enough for one single touch. She was willing to place all her hope in Jesus. The result? "*Immediately her bleeding stopped and she ... was freed from her suffering*" (v.29).

When Jesus asked who had touched Him, the disciples were confused, wondering how they could possibly know in such a large crowd, or why it would matter anyway. What they didn't know was this particular touch that Jesus felt was different—someone had touched him *in faith*, and He felt a miracle flow forth from Himself.

As a teenager, I was blessed to have spent time with a woman of similar faith, my Grandma Dinnick. While there are numerous miracles of provision, deliverance, and healing to retell, the desperation of this woman in the Bible reminds me of one miracle in particular that I witnessed. Grandma suffered for many years with a large abdominal hernia, kept in check by a wide elasticized type of medical band around the area. Surgery wasn't an option, as Grandma had a serious heart condition that prevented such procedures.

One Saturday afternoon, the lemon-sized hernia popped out of place. It had done this occasionally in the past. Dr. Scott was called, and he began many minutes of navigating around the hernia to put it back, but with no success. The prognosis was not good. He felt he had done all he could. As I stood by Grandma's bedside, she asked the doctor to simply lay his hands on the hernia once more and allow her to pray. In that prayer, Grandma reached out, in great faith, and touched the hem of His garment. All three of us watched that hernia slide back into place without effort. It was her moment of desperation, and Jesus responded to her faith. Jesus not only returned it to its rightful place but kept it there for the remaining eight years of her life.

Both of these women knew something we all should consider today. When you think you've reached the end of possibilities and there's nowhere else to turn, He's always there. When our hope is placed in Jesus—anything is possible.

Jesus, when it looks like I've tried everything and see no solution, give me the courage to press through to you in faith. Thank you that my story matters to you.

Wrestling with Our Faith

Day Two

"Why would you ever complain ... saying, 'God ... doesn't care what happens to me'? ... God doesn't come and go... He doesn't get tired out, doesn't pause to catch his breath. And... He energizes those who get tired, gives fresh strength to dropouts... those who wait upon God get fresh strength."

—Isaiah 40:27–30, MSG

God chose him to be a prophet before he was born. His ministry came at a time when Judah was at its worst, and it covered a period of forty years and five kings. Like Moses (Exodus 4:10), Jeremiah claimed an inability to do what God was asking. He considered himself too young and unable to speak. Jeremiah's objection to being a prophet was denied immediately by the Lord, as youth, inexperience, and lack of confidence are not acceptable disqualifiers.

Jeremiah's call was mainly as a prophet of doom while also one of restoration. He called upon people to turn, or repent, more than any other prophet. Still, the people didn't listen to him. Jeremiah wrestled with his faith and his call many times throughout his life. Doing what God asked brought him insults and reproach. He wept for the people who heard his message. When Jeremiah's faith waned, he tried not to preach the Word, but it became like a fire shut up in his bones. Then, weary and drained from the wrestling, he would begin preaching once again.

He was a prophet of God perpetually caught up in emotional turmoil. Plots were devised against his life, he was beaten, and even his fellow prophets were against him. Several times he asked God to deal with his enemies. The bottom line—he was serving God, walking in obedience, and what was happening to him just wasn't fair or just, but when faith grew, he praised God, prayed, and moved forward.

While most of us don't come close to the wrestle of Jeremiah, we all experience faith wrestles of our own—times when God doesn't make sense, doesn't seem fair, and seems to have let us down. It happened to me following the death of my mom—a lover of Jesus, full of compassion, rescuer of the lost, and prayer warrior. When Mom was in a care home later in life, feeding her was a tedious process. Nursing help was limited, so we hired a Christian lady from a local church to feed her lunch each weekday. Family would do weekends. The caregiver would report in with updates by phone, and we'd mail her a cheque. We were relieved that Mom was getting the attention she needed.

Mom made a glorious entrance to Heaven months later, and we held a celebration of her life. About two weeks after that, I received, with excitement, a letter from her hired caregiver. Finding out about additional special moments after a loved one passes is always comforting. Sadly, as I read the letter, I felt anger, resentment, and revenge seething deep inside. This caregiver's note was an admission that she had cashed all the cheques, lied during the many phone calls, and had only seen my mom for the first two weeks!

God and I had a wrestle. I wasn't ready to receive her "apology" or to forgive. I felt God should step in on our behalf to bring whatever justice we determined. I'm so glad God is loving, wise, and full of comfort. During the following few weeks, He helped me find the way back to faith through forgiveness and leaving the rest with Him. My strength was not found in the courage of my struggle but in the completeness of my surrender. Though painful, I was able to release the situation to Him and regain my freedom and joy.

God didn't give up on Jeremiah, and He didn't give up on me. When you're in a faith wrestle, God is patient. If you let Him, He'll show you the way to victory. In the long-term, wrestles build our faith and remind the enemy that the Greater One lives within!

Lord, it's true, I can find fresh strength in you. You're ready for my wrestles, and you'll show me the way to victory as I surrender, in faith, to you.

A Legacy of Faith

Day Three

Contributed by Judy Hampton

"Now faith brings our hopes into reality and becomes the foundation needed to acquire the things we long for. It is all the evidence required to prove what is still unseen. This testimony of faith is what previous generations were commended for."
—Hebrews 11:1–2, TPT

I remember the Sunday when the Pastor Cook looked at our family sitting in Vineland Pentecostal Church and said, "There are some faces we'll miss seeing next Sunday!" As an eight-year-old girl, I'd been aware of weekly meetings in our home involving fervent prayer. Foundational to those prayers was faith—faith to multiply, faith to share, faith to "add to the church" people who needed Him. The reality of answered prayer came to light as people gathered for the first church service at Lakeview Public School in the nearby town of Grimsby. Areas of leadership were established, newly arrived locals became involved, and a new congregation was birthed, officially named Grimsby Pentecostal Church, on October 19, 1965. Though just a child, the joy of this new adventure was stamped upon my heart.

Over the years, I saw my parents, John and Marg Dalgleish, serve God with humility and meekness. They sensed what God was doing, loved God's house, trusted their leadership, and were happy to serve wherever there was a need.

Mom shone brightest in the church foyer as a greeter. Clearly, she was anointed for the role! She was a lover of people, and many would seek her out for a heartfelt hug. Her memory for names and details was remarkable. At her funeral in July 2010, people spoke of how Mom's love, and her hugs, had impacted their lives. She imparted hope, comfort, value, and acceptance when people needed it most!

My dad was a familiar face in town, as he served on the local police force. He also had a heart for evangelism. In June 1966, when evening services were held in the Grimsby Plaza parking lot, he was truly in his element! The opportunity to worship, evangelize, and reach the people he served on a daily basis was a double blessing for him!

In the mid-90s when a sovereign move of the Holy Spirit came to the now renamed congregation, Lakemount Worship Centre, my parents were right on board with what God was doing. They activated their well-watered, ever-increasing faith in the God of breakthroughs as they prayed for those seeking a touch from God, a life transformation, a healing, or salvation. They loved lingering in the presence of God, and their prayer was, "More, Lord!"

Mom and Dad stood on the truth of Hebrews 11:6: *"And without faith living within us it would be impossible to please God. For we come to God in faith, knowing that he is real and that he rewards the faith of those who passionately seek him"* (TPT). We watched God respond to that faith in unprecedented ways. I've observed how a move of God can begin with ordinary people who are willing to pray and step out in faith. The legacy of faith that has been passed to all of us started with a vision from the Lord and a willingness to obey. Only eternity will unveil the full story of the transactions that have taken place, and still continue, because Mom and Dad and their group of pioneers said "yes" and stepped out *in faith*.

Lord, your Word says that a good person leaves an inheritance for their children's children (Proverbs 13:22). Teach me to be a person of faith who sets in motion a legacy of multiplied Kingdom investment that reaps eternal rewards. In Jesus' name.

Faith Shared

Day Four

Contributed by Catherine (Cathy) Ritson

"And I pray that as you share your faith with others it will grip their lives too, as they see the wealth of good things in you that come from Christ Jesus."
—Philemon 1:6, TLB

Corrie ten Boom, a woman who harboured hundreds of Jewish people in her home during World War II, describes faith in this way: "Faith sees the invisible, believes the unbelievable, and receives the impossible."[1]

My faith journey is a lifetime of events that continually illustrate God's ability to achieve what we're unable to see or imagine. Reflecting on my childhood brings tremendous joy to my heart. My parents shared their love for the Lord and their Christian values with us and others. Losing my father to cancer, however, was more than a small bump in the road. A dear friend suggested I try writing a prayer journal each day. Those times of quiet reflection brought peace, increasing my faith and an indwelling of the Lord's presence. My father's favourite verse, Matthew 11:28, brought hope and peace to my soul: *"Come to me, all you who are weary and burdened and I will give you rest."* As we rest in Him, our faith begins to flourish.

That same faith called my husband and me to a lifetime of church ministry and social work across Canada as pastors with The Salvation Army. While serving in Medicine Hat, Alberta, we visited a family from our congregation who lived in the country. Travelling home, I suffered a severe asthma attack and was placed on a breathing machine in hospital. But God kept

---

1   "Quotes by Corrie ten Boom," Grace Quotes, https://gracequotes.org/author-quote/corrie-ten-boom/, accessed July 17, 2021.

me safe, and He had a plan to use my faith in ways I couldn't have anticipated or imagined. At my moment of physical weakness, He was opening hearts so that I could share His gifts of love and mercy. A friend came to visit one evening and together we shared scripture and prayed the verse in Romans 8:28: *"And we know that in all things God works for the good of those who love him, who have been called according to his purpose."*

In the bed beside mine was a young teenager named Becky. The disease that raged throughout her was more than her frail body could handle. I awoke the next morning to find Becky sitting on her bed, facing me. "I want to know more about the words you were sharing last night. You seem so happy yet suffering and unable to breathe."

At that moment, I was reminded that God's plan never fails. We can trust Him to use us, if we are willing, in both sickness and health, in weakness or in strength. Over the next few days, I was blessed to witness Becky accept Christ as her personal Saviour.

Once recovered, I returned to visit Becky often, each time reading to her from her new Bible. We would share deep conversations, which also allowed Becky to lead her mother to faith in the Lord. Six weeks later, Becky left this world to be with the Lord she now knew and loved.

As Christians we're called to trust the Lord's timing, remain available, and reach out to a suffering world searching for answers. He knows when hearts are ready. Corrie ten Boom's faith was tested and proven in the most difficult circumstances and in her greatest moments of weakness, yet she believed. Cultivating the faith that was lovingly demonstrated to me has inspired me to share it with countless others. Faith changes us; it changes our hearts and gives us hope and a future. Choose faith in Christ and He will use your faith in ways you never anticipated.

Jesus, my deep desire is to love others the way you love me. Keep me attentive and aligned to the opportunities Heaven sends my way.

An Amazing Faith

Day Five

"Jesus was amazed. Turning to the crowd he said, 'Never among all the Jews in Israel have I met a man with faith like this.'"

—Luke 7:9, TLB

Life has a way of catching us off guard. A certain centurion (Luke 7) found himself with an unexpected problem with what looked like no solution. His highly valued servant was dying, and there was nothing further that could be done. The centurion was willing to risk whatever was needed to make a final effort to save him. He knew he could no longer deal with this.

The centurion heard that Jesus was in Capernaum, and being a Gentile and a Roman officer, he sent some elders of the Jews, rather than going himself, to ask Jesus to come and heal his servant. The elders pleaded with Jesus on the centurion's behalf and reminded Him how deserving this centurion was due to his investment in building the synagogue. Jesus' reaction was one of compassion. He said He would come with them to heal the boy. How shocking to the mostly Jewish crowd—He would go to the house of a Gentile, and a Roman at that!

But when Jesus wasn't far from the house, the centurion sent some more friends to cancel the visit! He didn't deserve to have Him come under his roof. He had them relay that his unworthiness had held him back from coming to ask for this favour directly. What happened to cause the centurion to change his mind and his ask? I think he wanted to make it clear that he knew who he was dealing with—the one who knew that there were lots of things on his résumé that the Jews didn't know about, that didn't fit the category of "deserving." He knew he had no right to be asking based on the favour he'd earned. He confessed his unworthiness.

But great faith says I can believe that God's love and actions on my behalf aren't based on my getting things right. God can make a way when I'm undeserving. The centurion realized that God could work regardless of the circumstances, so he said, *"Sir, don't inconvenience yourself by coming to my home, for I am not worthy . . . Just speak a word from where you are, and my servant boy will be healed!"* (Luke 7:7, TLB). He understood, as a man under authority, that Jesus didn't have to *come*; He wasn't boxed in to the "how." He had the authority to *speak a word*, and the sickness would go. The scripture says that when Jesus heard this, He was amazed at the centurion and said, *"I tell you, I have not found such great faith even in Israel"* (Luke 7:9). When the men returned to the house, they saw that the servant had been healed. That's the power of a word from the Lord! They may have expected that word to be "Be healed" or "Rise up," but He had spoken *a word*, and the servant was healed.

When we're up against a wall, the thing we need most is faith in God. When we hear a word from God, whether it's the word we're expecting or not, we must understand that God is moving in the situation in our lives. His word can transform, it can heal, it can bring hope. But we must have faith enough to let God do it His way. Real faith expects a "yes" but can endure a "no" or a different answer. When the centurion took off the restrictions, Jesus was amazed at his faith. We need never shout across the spaces to an absent God. He is nearer than our own soul, closer than our most secret thoughts.[2] Ask Him to help you grow a faith that amazes Him. Trust the word that He has for you.

Lord, I confess my unworthiness. I am so humbled when I consider the price you paid for my salvation. Help me to recognize your voice in a greater way, even when it speaks an unexpected word. Help me learn to have a faith that can endure a "no" or a different answer, trusting that you know best.

---

2   "70 Faith Strengthening Christian Quotes," Planet of Success, http://www.plane-tofsuccess.com/blog/2017/christian-quotes/, accessed August 2, 2021.

Focused Faith

Day Six

"For this reason I am telling you, whatever things you ask for in prayer [in accordance with God's will], believe [with confident trust] that you have received them, and they will be given to you."

—Mark 11:24, AMP

It was a frigid, stormy January afternoon when my Uncle Gordon stepped out of his house, bundled up with winter boots, toque, and some well-worn gloves. He had business to do with his Father, and it required privacy. There would be possible groanings and questions not suited for the family audience. The nation's depression had hit hard, and sacrifice was familiar. But this one was too close to the heart. His sweet little girl was turning four, and she expected God was going to send her a birthday cake.

The bitter cold penetrated his bones, and his body shivered as his feet made their way along the crusty driveway. As the large flakes burned against his face, he lifted his hands to Heaven and cried out, "God, Winnie is counting on you to send the cake. I'm afraid if I can't get one, she'll never believe again." He was a man of faith and prayer, but in that moment, he knew he was asking for the impossible.

As he poured out his petition, he heard a loud bang. Making his way through the strong winds and blizzard, he discovered that a truck had hit a bump at the intersection and had slid partway into the ditch. Retrieving a shovel and some sand, he went to work helping the driver get back on track. Shouting a thank you through the wind, the driver motioned him back to the truck as they finished. He opened the back door. It was a bakery truck returning from its daily deliveries—primarily empty! The driver handed Uncle Gordon the single box that remained. Inside was the fanciest chocolate cake ever—decorated and ready for a birthday!

Sometimes faith must be exercised even for cakes! God has actually been answering faith-filled "cake requests" for a few thousand years. In the time of the prophet Elijah, there was a famine in the land. Elijah had been running from the angry King Ahab, but God had been directing him to safety. As the famine escalated, Elijah was led by the Lord to the village of Zarephath. There he met a widow who had been exercising her faith for oil and flour cakes every day for the past two years. She was now gathering sticks to build a fire and bake the final meal for herself and her son. It "appeared" that her efforts to provide for herself and her son had, in the end, finally proven futile. A meagre bit of oil and flour remained. Elijah instructed her, *"Fear not; go and do as you have said; but first make me a little cake of it and bring it to me, and afterward make for yourself and your son"* (1 Kings 17:13, RSV).

Imagine the conversation she must have had with God! But Elijah delivered a promise from God—if she would simply believe and respond in faith, her bin of flour and jar of oil would never run out until the day the famine was over. She did as directed, and God continued to provide cakes for three years for Elijah, the widow, and her son until the famine ended.

When you're facing an impossibility, God cares. Nothing is too great or too small. Our Father has provided water from a rock, sent dinners carried by ravens, given rain in a drought, multiplied meal and oil, and even dropped off chocolate birthday cake. Your prayers of faith are heard by Heaven. God's resources are limitless. Activating obedient faith can release your most significant breakthrough. As you trust Him, you can expect His provision and a few surprises just when you need them most.

Lord, your resources are limitless. Help me to exercise faith in ways I haven't yet considered. Thank you for reminding me that my life matters to you, and you are ready to hear my prayers.

An Unbroken Gaze

Day Seven

Contributed by Matt Tapley

"So we fix our eyes not on what is seen, but on what is unseen, since what is seen is temporary, but what is unseen is eternal."

—2 Corinthians 4:18

A.W. Tozer said that faith is the unbroken gaze of the soul on Jesus.[3] This is the best definition of faith I've ever found. And it was this definition that began to heal my heart during an incredibly painful and challenging season in my life.

I came across this quotation while reading Tozer's classic book, *The Pursuit of God*, when my wife and I were on a vacation in Florida. Though a Florida vacation may seem restful and easy, beneath the surface I was processing incredible disappointment and heartache. Our youngest daughter had recently passed away after a three-year battle with cancer.

We had just come through the fight of our lives, frankly, feeling as though we had lost. Sleepless nights and hospital stays. Numerous surgeries. Chemo. Radiation. Transfusions and countless treatments—both conventional and naturopathic—and yet our daughter was no longer with us. Sarah was in Heaven before her twelfth birthday. We had two other kids at home, a growing church in the middle of a building program, and the responsibility of living out our response to grief and loss before a watching community.

We were tired.

I was numb.

Life was moving forward, but I was frozen in place.

---

3   A.W. Tozer, *The Pursuit of God* (Bloomington, MN: Bethany House, 2013), 57.

I had a world of questions and pain mixed with a mountain of responsibilities and concerns. When Sarah was diagnosed with Stage 4 cancer, I wrestled with God: "Lord, you can heal her. I believe you can. How can I believe it any more intently than I already do?" Yet her healing never came. When Sarah passed away, my heart was broken. My questions became: "Lord, did I somehow not believe purely enough? How did this happen? How does faith actually *work*?"

While sitting on that Florida beach and reading Tozer's words, it was like the Holy Spirit shone a light on every scripture that describes faith using the metaphor of sight. I began to realize that faith keeps an unbroken gaze on Jesus not to get a result, but to remain properly focused on Him regardless of what happens.

> *Therefore we do not lose heart. Though outwardly we are wasting away, yet inwardly we are being renewed day by day. For our light and momentary troubles are achieving for us an eternal glory that far outweighs them all. So we fix our eyes not on what is seen, but on what is unseen, since what is seen is temporary, but what is unseen is eternal.*
>
> —2 Corinthians 4:16–18

I think I was losing heart. My "outward" circumstance of an intense health battle followed by tragedy had become an internal struggle of doubt and turmoil. But I began to understand that if I could fix my eyes on Jesus, I could see beyond my circumstance and have an internal reality that was in direct contrast to my external circumstance. Paul calls it *"fixing your eyes on the unseen."* What we cannot see is more real and significant than the visible realm. This is the very definition of faith.

Faith isn't defined by what it does. Faith is beholding Jesus no matter what. For me, refocusing my heart on who Jesus is began an inner renewal by reminding me that He's not only a healer of bodies, but He is a healer of hearts.

Faith doesn't lead me to avoid pain and adversity; instead, it leads me through it and teaches me how to overcome—even in loss. Faith gives me a perspective beyond the temporary and visible. It opens the eyes of my heart to see Jesus above and beyond my pain.

Whatever may be trying to cloud *your* soul's gaze upon Jesus, let me encourage you to turn the eyes of your heart upon Him. Consider His promises as a student. Meditate on His nature as a friend. And feast upon His presence as a worshipper.

Lord, today you're inviting me to look to you, but I confess that sometimes my vision is clouded by pain, doubt, and disappointment. I want your heart to be my dwelling place, and your love to heal my heart. I lift my eyes above the temporary to see the eternal, and I feast upon your presence.

Obedient Faith

Day Eight

It was through faith that Noah, on receiving God's warning of impending disaster, reverently constructed an ark to save his household. This action of faith condemned the unbelief of the rest of the world, and won for Noah the righteousness before God which follows such a faith.

—Hebrews 11:7, PHILLIPS

Noah wasn't perfect, but he walked in a way that brought pleasure to God. Nothing pleases God more than to see someone walking by faith and making their decisions based on their relationship with Him. This is exceptionally amazing when you discover the degree to which evil had infiltrated and gripped the culture. In fact, God was disappointed that He had created humanity.

Noah was five hundred years of age when he received very specific instructions from God to build an ark of safety. God was sending a flood to destroy the great evil in the land. Although rain was not a known entity in his day, over the next 120 years, he stayed focussed on the plan that God had entrusted to him. Noah walked in obedient faith with every swing of the axe against another tree of gopherwood, with every question in his mind about what a flood would look like. He worked and he witnessed while the bystanders mocked. The task was formidable, but it was his heavenly Father's affirmation and trust that undergirded his faith for this project with its elusive finish line.

Even after the completion of the ark itself, there was much to do to prepare for the flood. There was the task of rounding up the list of clean and unclean beasts, birds, and every creeping thing and getting all of those animals into the ark (even if they were supernaturally compliant). Then there was the faith required to estimate the amount of food necessary for this unknown period of time. But Noah walked with God! That doesn't mean any part of the task was easy—it simply means that he heard from God and obeyed at every step. If you don't walk close to God, obedience can be an irritation, but when you're close enough to hear His whispers and feel His heartbeat, obedience becomes a joy.

Once the boat was filled with Noah's family and the animals, the Lord closed the door behind them. When the Lord tells us to move forward in obedience to His promptings, He may close the door behind us to prevent our return to a previous or completed season. This is for our protection. If Noah had walked back for another look, or just to be certain he'd heard from God, he and the entire family and animals would have drowned. When the door of the ark was shut, he had to remain in faith for another forty days and nights during the deluge of rain. It wasn't until nine months after the journey began that the ark came to rest on Mount Ararat.

Noah's life was characterized by radical obedience and righteousness in a climate of pressure, immorality, unbelief, and mockery, yet he exhibited profound faith as he worked and worshipped, watching for the fulfilment of God's plan. It's important to act upon our faith in God's direction for us, no matter the cost. It may look foolish, it may go against the culture of our day, it may bring rejection, and it may leave us feeling alone. But as the word we receive is worked out by faith, we live larger, find fulfillment in our purpose, and see the promises of God manifest in our lives. Today, hear the voice of the Spirit challenging you to say yes to being one who walks with God in unwavering obedience. Don't turn back. Faith in Him will not disappoint. You will obtain the promise!

Holy Spirit, I want to be one who walks in patient, radical obedience and righteousness in a climate of pressure, rejection, and loneliness. May my faith stand strong despite the cost when the task isn't easy and I don't understand. Teach me to boast in you, Lord, and walk as an overcomer. In Jesus' name.

Holding Fast

Day Nine

Contributed by Shirley Brown

"Let us hold fast the profession of our faith without wavering; (for he is faithful that promised;)"

—Hebrews 10:23, KJV

"And Abraham said. . . the lad and I will go yonder and worship, and we will come back to you."

—Genesis 22:5, NKJV (emphasis added)

Saturday, August 3, 1968, began like many other summer days—hot and sticky but with time to enjoy a leisurely breakfast with my husband, Ross, before he left for work. I had made a personal commitment to Jesus Christ two years earlier, and my heart was full of love for God, my husband, and our four children. I could never have anticipated how that day would unfold.

That was the day our twelve-year-old son, Robbie, went missing, never to be seen again. Robbie had left to do his papers about 4:00 p.m., but by 6:30 p.m., he still wasn't home. By 9:00 p.m., we had two policemen in our kitchen taking information and asking unending questions. As morning dawned, police and locals joined in a search. The police thought he may have drowned, but dragging operations of nearby waterways failed to turn up any evidence. They thought perhaps he had run away, but that made no sense. He hadn't taken a coat or his money, and he was excited about a new afterschool job stocking shelves at Canadian Tire, where his dad worked. The remaining alternative was too horrifying. I fell on my knees and prayed: "Father, please don't let anyone hurt my baby. You take him. Our hope is in you, not in this world."

In the early days of his disappearance, we were never left alone. The consistent, calming faith of our supportive friends and relatives helped to replenish us when we were at our weakest. When we were numb and despondent, their love and presence carried us.

Over the years, there have been many "sightings" and false alarms. Each new possibility has brought hope … and then … more disappointment. Though God's comfort is always available, sometimes our hearts simply become weary of the journey. I learned to visit my Strong Tower, pour out my complaint to Him, and remember His faithfulness. Though it's hard, we have to cultivate faith even in barren lands so that we don't remain there.

In 2006, the history of the tragedy was printed in the local newspaper: "Son Still Missing." The local police seemed unaware of the story. How devastating it was to find out that Robbie's case file hadn't been transferred from paper to electronic mode. It had become not just "cold" but non-existent. The sense of abandonment was deep. But God!

When the file was eventually found, the police asked me for forgiveness, admitting they "had dropped the ball." Just when I felt that the ground beneath me had stabilized and life was feeling "normal," I had more forgiving to deal with (Mark 11:25). I knew forgiveness would free me from the power of this situation over me, and with God's help, I forgave.

Although still without closure today, God continues to give me peace and a faith to tell others of His keeping power. Heaven knows the details that we don't, and I hold on to God's promise that I will see my son one day soon. Although the journey has been pain-filled and so difficult, I am now in my eighty-fifth year and still walking out my faith in Jesus, going strong for Him. I give God all the glory. Proverbs 3:5–6 encourages me daily as I trust Him, assured that He is directing my path.

Lord, sometimes the questions without answers become unbearable. Thank you for this testimony of unwavering faith that reminds me that I can face anything when I keep my eyes on you.

Unshakeable Faith

Day Ten

"The path we walk is charted by faith, not by what we see with our eyes."
—2 Corinthians 5:7, VOICE

Grandma (yes, the same "Desperate Faith" grandma from Day One) was a woman of thriving faith and abundant love. Grandma's faith was the strength in the fabric of her everyday life. There was no wavering, no doubt, no self-pity, no worry about "what ifs," but only declarations of the goodness of God and what she anticipated He would be doing "very soon."

Grandpa was a Methodist minister who preached a circuit on Sundays—three congregations in the Mono Mills and Orangeville areas. He would preach the closest one in the morning, sometimes bringing Grandma home before visiting the additional two churches. Since the travel was by horse and buggy, Sundays were exhausting. They shared a resolute faith and expectation of how God would meet people at each service, and on Sunday evenings the two of them would review and enjoy the testimonies of God's faithfulness at each service.

On this particular Sunday night, Grandpa was late coming home. Grandma wasn't sure why. The list of potential reasons eluded her. She prepared for bed and fell off to sleep. A short time later, she was awakened with a start, sat up in bed, and felt the burden of the Lord to pray. She began to pray fervently, noting the lateness of the hour, declaring the promises of God over his life and his journey home, and over anyone he might be ministering to at the time. When she felt peace, she went back to sleep.

About three hours later, Grandpa arrived home, alive and well! It turned out that just a few miles away there had been a sudden and severe rainstorm. The thunder, lightning, and torrential downpours had delayed his departure from the final church service. Even as he left, many of the roads were drenched, the winds were still strong, and visibility was limited.

He was making good progress when suddenly his horse rose up with a loud neighing and stopped in its tracks, sending Grandpa forward and almost over the buggy's edge. He prodded the horse to move along, but the horse repeated his response. He would not move. Grandpa got out to see what was wrong. He recognized that they were at the entry to the wooden bridge that crossed the stream, a stream that was now swollen and raging. While standing there, Grandpa realized that the stream had actually overflowed the bridge, taking it out completely. Had the horse continued, Grandpa, horse, and buggy would have been swallowed up by the torrent.

Grandma relayed to him what had happened after she had fallen asleep, how the Lord had awakened her to pray. "What time was it when the horse stopped?" she asked. Yes! It was at the exact time that Grandma had been praying. Corrie ten Boom once said, "Faith is like radar that sees through the fog—the reality of things at a distance that the human eye cannot see."[4]

Grandma "saw" a need for exercising faith, and she responded. In spite of not knowing the situation, she knew that the same God who had formed the universe, parted the Red Sea waters, and delivered bread to her empty cupboards was well able to care for whatever Grandpa was facing. And she was right! Her faithful God had no problem halting a horse. Grandma had an active, unshakeable confidence in her God that had no limits. May the Lord teach us to embrace His presence to dispel any worry or doubt and invite peace, protection, and joy.

Jesus, I'm asking you to help me grow in this kind of unwavering faith! I want to know your amazing peace when I don't have an answer. Help me to remember that you've got my back!

---

4 "Top 27 Christian Quotes about Faith," Godtube, https://www.godtube.com/news/top-27-christian-quotes-about-faith.html, accessed July 1, 2021.

Faith: Tried, Tested, and Purified

Day Eleven

Contributed by Carl and Heide Villeseche

"These trials will show that your faith is genuine. It is being tested as fire tests and purifies gold—though your faith is far more precious than mere gold. So when your faith remains strong through many trials, it will bring you much praise and glory and honor on the day when Jesus Christ is revealed to the whole world."

—I Peter 1:7, NLT

Selfish decisions, self-centredness, loss of vitality, patience worn thin—all of it was enough for us to determine our marriage was done. Christians? Yes. Faith? Yes. Willingness to work on this together? Finished. We decided to separate, not knowing what was ahead. At the time, we didn't love anyone but ourselves, and life had become very superficial and challenging. There wasn't much left to enjoy. It was the hardest thing each of us had ever faced. Painful, turbulent, humiliating. We had both come to the end of ourselves.

While journeying through this crisis, we each had to draw on our own personal faith in God and, separately, decided to pursue Him instead of pursuing what was lost, or looking for something to replace it. As we pressed in, God met each of us uniquely, and a brand-new revelation of our significance in Him began. Daily, He began to bathe us in His unfailing love. We became aware of our self-focused thinking and actions and heard the call to make Him Lord. We learned that faith is really the courage to let God take control!

It's a huge revelation when you begin to comprehend the value He places on you personally, especially when those around you may be saying otherwise. Recognizing that it was God's opinion of us that mattered brought a sense of freedom. We began to believe and trust that what He says is truth! We no longer had to prove our worth because it was established at Calvary. No one could ever love us more, and God would never love us less. We didn't need to entrust others with the measurement of our worth or depend on one another to affirm that worth. It rested in the hands of our loving heavenly Father.

The Holy Spirit alerted us to many lies that we had believed. We chose to repent for believing those lies that brought insecurity and discord. Some had come from listening to the voices of those around us, some from words we had spoken to each other, and some from words we had spoken to ourselves. It was time to rest in who we were in Him, stop self-focusing, and begin to boast in the Lord (Psalm 34:2)! That's the language of faith! With that decision and declaration, a dramatic change became evident.

To our great surprise, while we were each pursuing God and receiving some wise counsel, He provided opportunity for us to "find" one another again. It was truly a miracle of grace and restoration. God did exceedingly abundantly more than we had ever asked or imagined! We didn't expect Him to spark a new love—we hadn't planned for it or asked for it! We were simply continuing our faith journeys with Him, repenting from the behaviour that caused the split in the first place, and re-establishing some priorities in our lives. While we did our part, God did His and brought a supernatural healing in our relationship.

In the decade and a half since, our marriage has continued to flourish. We've witnessed how the healing has impacted our children, extended family, and even friends. We're learning to lean into God and have found that the quicker we are to turn to Him, the greater our peace in difficult times. God, let your praises be ever on our lips, for you are always faithful and an anchor for our lives!

Lord, show me any lies that are distorting the truth of who I am and who you are. I choose truth. Help me to build healthier relationships as you set me free from any self-focus and heal my heart.

Faith for the Furnace

Day Twelve

"When you pass through the waters, I am with you; when you pass through the streams, they will not overwhelm you. When you walk through the fire, you will not be burned; the flames will not harm you."

—Isaiah 43:2, NET

King Nebuchadnezzar was a man with seriously misplaced passion. When Daniel had successfully interpreted his troubling dreams, the king declared that Daniel's God was the God of gods, and he made Daniel ruler over Babylon. He appointed Daniel's three friends and intercessors, Shadrach, Meshach, and Abednego, to assist. Nebuchadnezzar celebrated by building a massive statue of gold before which everyone was to fall in worship. (If you grew up on Veggie Tales, it was "the Bunny, the Bunny").

As Nebuchadnezzar scanned the horizon, he saw people of many nationalities bowing down to the image he had made, and he was pleased. But when he received word that Shadrach, Meshach, and Abednego refused to bow, he flew into a rage and threatened to throw them into a raging furnace. These three, however, were walking in a deep devotion to God, and their faith was in Him. They believed God would protect and deliver them from the king's threats, but their faith wasn't dependent on the expected outcome. Their faith was fastened to the one who was fighting on their behalf, *whether or not He saved them from the furnace* (Daniel 3:16–17).

Fully clothed and bound, Shadrach, Meshach, and Abednego were delivered to the furnace. They felt the intensity of the heat and saw those who carried them die from that heat, but their hearts remained steadfast.

Imagine the king's disbelief when he looked into the flames and saw four men, not three, walking around unharmed and unbound! The preincarnate Christ stood with those three faith-filled courageous followers of the true God! On that day, Nebuchadnezzar saw the infinite difference between the God of Israel and the idol he had fashioned. Before his bedazzled eyes, God performed a great miracle. Shadrach, Meshach, and Abednego walked out of that furnace—not even a hair on their heads singed by the flames, with no smell of smoke, free and unbound.

God often delivers us from having to face the furnace, but sometimes He delivers us *in* the furnace, and those are often the greatest faith-cultivating moments in our lives. I think one of the challenges we must face is furnace-avoidance: "God, deliver me from facing this test. Don't make me share my views on biblical marriage. Don't let the boss assign me to that task." Sometimes we want to avoid even low-level flames. But Jesus knows that the furnace is a place where we will grow, mature, and be loosed from the things that have us bound. If these three had given up in fear, they would have missed an adventure with Him that marked them for eternity with new levels of faith, favour, and authority.

Maybe difficult times in the presence of God are worth the risk. Is there anything greater than His presence? So often we go through life for days at a time without a consciousness of the Lord's presence with us. But when trouble comes, when the flames lick at our feet, when life presses in on us, then we discover that Jesus is right by our side and has been the entire time.

Every second you spend wishing God would take away a struggle is a forfeited opportunity to overcome.[5] What God said to Shadrach, Meshach, Abednego, Stephen, Paul, and Corrie ten Boom is what He still says to you today: "Hold fast to your faith and I'll meet you in the furnace."

Holy Spirit, I love your presence more than deliverance, more than my comforts of life, more than an easier path. Strengthen me to stand true when things get hot. In Jesus' name.

---

5   "Steven Furtick Quotes," Love Expands, "https://loveexpands.com/quotes/steven-fur-tick-803139/, accessed August 25, 2021.

When Faith Explodes

Day Thirteen
Contributed by Ken and Amie Vandevrie

"Seek the Kingdom of God above all else, and he will give you everything you need."
—Luke 12:31, NLT

At church one evening in 2004, we were asked, "If there was no limit to your money, what would you do with it?" The thought was shocking, especially for a couple struggling financially. Imagining having "more than enough" wasn't something we had even considered. While we held truth in tension—yes, our Father "owned the cattle on a thousand hills"—we also knew we needed to get out of debt. This would be wise stewardship. At the same time, we hadn't allowed room for faith or dreams. We wondered, with a God like ours, "Is there even a limit?"

Unable to sleep that night, I got up to pray, waiting on Him to show me His idea of a faith goal that wasn't just my flesh. I got out my journal of prophetic encouragements that Ken and I had received over the past few years, and as I read, a picture of a property with two buildings set in an L came across my mind. One building had a row of windows with hands waving out of them—I sensed they were people God wanted us to help. This was a stretch. Could it be God? We were believing for freedom from debt, but this was beyond my faith reach!

We'd been searching for a place to move our studio business/home for some time. Ken's dad found the perfect house that already had a studio in it, and it was in the exact area we were hoping for. The newspaper ad said that the price tag was $1.2 million, and we were beyond broke. I heard clearly in my spirit, "Do you have the faith to believe I could *give* this to you?" I remember responding, "Well, it would only be you who could!" Ken called just to inquire. The answer? Only if we were pre-approved for $1 million could we even see it. What a laugh! Of course we weren't. So we waited, but with a hope and a faith that was now willing to dream of Heaven's possibilities. For months we continued asking the agent about it, but it didn't sell! Finally, the seller, now desperate, allowed us to come for a personal tour!

As we drove onto the property, I saw two houses positioned in an L, exactly as in the vision. Faith exploded in my heart, and I knew God was going to supply for our business in a very *big* way. He had shown Himself to me in impossible situations before, just not a $1.2 million one! That day, Ken connected with the owner, they became friends, and an amazing deal and a whole bunch of God's favour happened! We moved in July 2006, just two years after the vision! The agent said in his twenty-five years of doing real estate, he hadn't seen anything like this. The month we moved in, the finances started coming in—God's miraculous provision.

Four years ago, we decided to sell the additional house, but we couldn't due to a problem with its boundary line. That was disappointing, as it would have been the last thing needed to reach our debt-free goal. *Only God knew* that *now*, four years later, that property would double in value, and that extra house would be worth what we paid for both! As I write this article, the boundary problem solved, we sit on the edge of that sale—watching His soon to be fulfilled promise to "give" us that house and property that we saw in the ad. We're now better positioned to respond to those waving hands, and we've already begun! Together, we've learned that if we wait on Him and keep Him as our focus, nothing will be impossible. "The issue of faith is not so much whether we believe in God, but whether we believe the God we believe in."[6]

Lord, my spirit is filled with the joy of victory. Help me to remember that you are always working on my behalf, even when I don't see it, and teach me to dream again with eyes of faith.

---

6   R. C. Sproul, "20 Fantastic Christian Quotes about Faith, Viral Believer, https://viralbeliever.com/christian-quotes-about-faith/, accessed August 5, 2021.

Seeing Differently

Day Fourteen
Contributed by Dayo Adeyemo

*"Joshua ... and Caleb ... who were among those who had explored the land ...
and said ... 'The land we passed through and explored is exceedingly good. If the
Lord is pleased with us, he will lead us into that land ... and will give it to us
... do not be afraid of the people of the land, because we will devour them ...
the Lord is with us ...'"*

—Numbers 14:6–9

Numbers 13 and 14 tell the story of how believers ought to see. There's something about seeing that grows the Christian faith. Leaders were selected in Israel to go and spy out the promised land that God had sworn to them through Abraham. This reconnaissance survey strategy is relevant to us today—it gives structure to how we're meant to live our lives and walk by faith. It's all about seeing! All of the spies saw something, but obviously many did not see what God expected them to see. The Bible says we ought to walk by faith and not by sight.

The story reveals that they saw the land flowing with milk and honey—they even brought evidence of the luscious fruit of the land—but they saw also the challenges. The children of Anak were strong, and the great cities were walled. They also saw people who had no covenant with God. They saw the Hittites, Jebusites, and Canaanites. Caleb and Joshua, however, were different. They saw what God expected them to see. They injected the faith of God into the operation, allowing what God said to prevail, and they concluded that they were stronger.

Reporting what you see without seeing it through the Word of God gives birth to what I call grasshopper mentality. In Numbers 13:32, the spies describe themselves as grasshoppers, and in *their* sight, they were.

At one point, God said that He'd had enough murmuring against Himself, Joshua, and Moses. The Israelites were reminded not to rebel against the Lord. Joshua said "*. . . do not fear the people of the land, for they are bread for us. Their protection is removed from them, and the Lord is with us; do not fear them*" (Numbers 14:9, ESV). But the people did not yield. God affirmed Caleb as a man with "a different spirit" because he fully trusted the Lord. This is what it means to see differently.

There was a time in my life when I never saw things the way God wanted me to see them, but as I grew in faith, I learned to change my perspective. When my wife was five-months pregnant with our first child, she started bleeding. We saw blood, but we both decided to see it differently, to exercise faith. Even though in the natural things didn't look good, we weren't ready to give up. We pressed through to see the situation through God's promises. We confessed life and hope, knowing that it was all in God's hands, and we could fully trust Him with His response. God intervened, and all praise to Him, the pregnancy was sustained.

If you are in a challenging situation that is causing you to feel hopeless, don't simply rely on what you see. As you rely on His promises, you will realize that you are not a grasshopper facing a giant. He is on your side. Whatever the outcome, let the Word of God be the final authority. Above all, do not fear—the Lord is with you. Your response to impossibilities will change when seen from God's perspective.

Lord God, I desire to view my challenges with a new perspective, allowing your Word to be the final authority. You are with me, and I will not give place to fear because of the size of the problem—I choose to put my trust in you.

My Source: God's Power

Day Fifteen
Contributed by Paul Richardson

"so that your faith might not rest on human wisdom, but on God's power."

—I Corinthians 2:5

We receive vast amounts of information daily, and it can feel overwhelming, especially as it floods us from many sources. This information can be fact-based or opinion-based and can even be untrue. This information can form the basis for our decisions and actions, and ultimately our confidence.

I wrestle with this regularly as each day passes. What is our source? What is our foundation? Where is our confidence? Do I base my life on information that may or may not be true? Do I form my decisions on human wisdom that changes frequently? Does the loudest volume of information capture my attention?

In the verse above, the Apostle Paul's intention was to ground us in God's divine power, not in human wisdom. He came with results and not with words alone. If my faith depends on shrewd reasoning, it can be demolished by a more compelling argument, but faith produced by the power of God can never be overcome.

I love the Bible and find my source there. In Exodus 14, Moses and the people of God were facing a very difficult situation: being pursued by an angry army and being forced into an unforgiving sea. Information was pressing them on every side, but *"... when the Israelites saw the mighty hand of the Lord displayed ... the people feared the Lord and put their trust in him ..."* (v. 31).

I'm privileged to work with national Christian leadership teams in more than forty nations, and I frequently hear similar examples of the power of God. One time when I was in Eastern Europe, I met a church planter with one leg and a deformed arm. His mother had tried to abort him and failed, but it left him horribly disfigured. But as he was born and grew older, he was wonderfully transformed by the living Christ. Now in his fifties, he longed to see nearby villages and witness for Christ. So he travelled every week to the next village, seven kilometres away, by bicycle, with one leg, so that he could share the Good News of Jesus Christ. This is beyond human wisdom and is such evidence that our faith in Him will release His power in ways far beyond what we could imagine.

My encounter with that man changed me and gave me a different perspective, and perhaps it will do the same for you. Human decisions, actions, and wisdom are not our source and do not define us. Our faith, resting on God's power in our life, is transformational. God's power in our circumstance eclipses everything else.

Heavenly Father, I long to see your power displayed in my life. Take me beyond reasoning to a faith with a foundation resting on your power. I'm looking to you as I grow my faith. Change my perspective. You are a mighty God!

When Faith Fights

Day Sixteen

Contributed by Joe Courtney

"And the Lord said, . . . 'Indeed, Satan has asked for you, that he may sift you as wheat. But I have prayed for you, that your faith should not fail; and when you have returned to Me, strengthen your brethren.'"

—Luke 22:31–32, NKJV

"Those who sow in tears shall reap in joy."

—Psalm 126:5

Mothers are some of God's most powerful weapons, especially when they exercise a fighting faith to interrupt the plans of the enemy. Imagine the trust in God that the mother of Moses must have had when she placed his little basket in the Nile. For Hannah, it must have taken all the faith she could muster to drop Samuel off at the temple to be raised by Eli. In the mothers' hall of faith, add my mom, Marjorie Courtney.

Often I would see my mother on her knees, with Bible open, talking with God in her quiet way. I knew her prayers included me, but I was too numb to respond. I'm sure it was hard for her to keep believing when she saw me repeatedly making bad choices. The enemy is a thief who comes to steal, kill, and destroy (John 10:10), and that's what he was doing in my life. For years I believed that I didn't belong. I wasn't sure why, but I earned my dad's wrath emotionally and physically on a regular basis. (Of course, when I spray painted his Volkswagen red while he was at work … well, I get it!) Praying mothers fight with persistent faith and refuse to give up. Sadly, fear and lies can speak louder than kindness if the heart is wounded.

I left home before the age of fifteen, caught up in a lifestyle of excessive drinking, partying, and fighting. A beautiful, gentle, faith-filled aunt and uncle rescued me for a season during my high school years and got me through to graduation. I trained to be a paramedic. It was a great job, but often I was too hungover to drive. I was regularly assigned to cleaning the vehicles until one day when my boss dropped the bomb. I had to get help for my alcohol addiction in order to return to work. My marriage was a mess. I was unfaithful, and life had no meaning. I hit rock bottom. And where was my mother? Still on her knees.

God had given Mom a vision of me that was different from what anyone else, including myself, saw or believed. Mom stood in faith on God's Word, sowing for a great harvest, which included my salvation. So when I hit bottom, God was there, waiting for me. Mom had arranged it years earlier while on her knees. On a Friday night in 1979, my younger brother, "Pastor Howard," helped me battle the armies of Hell and find my way to Jesus. As the sun came up the next morning, I knew something had changed. I went to church that Sunday, where the leaders anointed me with oil and prayed. By the power of God, I was instantly and miraculously delivered from my addiction with no withdrawal! I have never turned back.

Mom never had much of anything, but she gave everything. She never shamed me or adjusted her level of love based on my behaviour. She continued to pray for me as I began a faith journey that eventually led to forgiveness between myself and my dad. God redeemed a loveless marriage and grew it into a fifty-year commitment with my God-fearing, forgiving wife.

If you're a praying mom, don't give up: "*The effectual fervent prayer of a righteous man (or woman) availeth much*" (James 5:16b, KJV, parentheses added). I'm so grateful for my mother's faith that fought for my freedom—it's a legacy that keeps me serving others, committed to His plans and purposes, and walking daily in freedom and joy.

Father, I'm reminded that some breakthroughs take longer than we anticipate. Put a fight in my spirit for those I love who have not yet found you. Thank you for those who have fought in prayer for me.

Faith in the Storm

Day Seventeen

But when you ask him, be sure that your faith is in God alone. Do not waver, for a person with divided loyalty is as unsettled as a wave of the sea that is blown and tossed by the wind.

—James 1:6, NLT

Despite their expertise as fishermen, no amount of seamanship could have prepared the disciples for the test of faith during the storm that they faced that night (Matthew 14:22–36; Mark 6:45–56; John 6:16–24). The more they rowed, the more the waves crashed against their boat. Travelling across the Sea of Galilea to Capernaum for over seven hours, they had only gone three or four miles. They were in survival mode—exhausted, desperate, and losing hope.

Around the "fourth watch," with the waves spilling into the boat and the winds pushing them in every direction, a figure appeared, coming toward them and walking on the water! They were so frightened they believed they were seeing a ghost. But Jesus spoke: *"Take courage! It is I. Do not be afraid"* (Matthew 14:27, ESV).

Peter doubted what he saw and asked Jesus to verify it was Him by inviting him onto the water as well. When Jesus did so, Peter stepped out of the boat and walked on the water, just like Jesus ... well, until he allowed the storm to influence his faith. When he took his eyes off Jesus, he began to sink. Jesus reached out to Peter, saved him, and they *stepped into the boat*. The storm stopped, and they immediately found themselves at their destination.

This rescue by Jesus sealed the deal for the disciples—they worshipped Him and declared, "*Truly you are the Son of God*" (Matthew 14:33, ESV).

This passage reminds me of a different sort of storm that took place one night in a Niagara hospital room. I was asked to sit for the night with an adult daughter of one of our church families while they went home for some rest. The daughter had been battling cancer and, now unresponsive, was maintaining life supported by medical devices. She had visited the church often but lacked a relationship with Christ. As I read scriptures and sang quietly, I prayed earnestly that somehow God would reach her. I was determined to keep rowing. The destination—her salvation.

At about 3:00 a.m. (the "fourth watch") something bumped my knee. I was paralyzed with shock as I observed that her hand had slid off the bed and onto my lap. As I began to reposition it, her eyes opened! At that moment, I felt like those disciples who thought they had seen a ghost. Though startled, I leaned in, praying through the sinner's prayer. I placed her hand back on the bed and she closed her eyes. *I knew that He had stepped into the boat!*

When the family arrived at 6:00 a.m., I left for a quick shower and rest, returning about noon. As I entered the room, I was heartsick to see them standing by her empty bed. I moved closer to offer condolences, and then, to my utter amazement, I saw her sitting in a chair, in hospital garb, but fully awake. Not only had Jesus stilled the storm and brought salvation, but He had made himself known for who He was and is—the Son of God, our Saviour, Healer, and Deliverer. No one could explain where the cancer had gone or how it happened, but days later, she went home to live additional years—saved, healed, and serving God.

I am humbled that God can take such little faith and use it to help execute heaven's plan and unleash the supernatural. I can't say that I doubted He *could* fully restore her, I just never thought to ask. My heart burned for her salvation, but that encounter taught me that I don't have to waver or be afraid. In the face of any storm, I can, in faith, believe big and ask big.

Lord, there are some stormy situations in my life right now. I invite you to step into my boat. I'm choosing to let go of doubt and fear, exercise my faith, and ask big.

Faith for Generosity

Day Eighteen

Give generously and generous gifts will be given back to you, shaken down to make room for more. Abundant gifts will pour out upon you with such an overflowing measure that it will run over the top! The measurement of your generosity becomes the measurement of your return.

—Luke 6:38, TPT

It was the third year of what would become, for many years, a team mission of sixteen passionate Jesus lovers to the schools of St. Lucia. During our week on the island, we would visit thirty-five schools with drama, music, and a gospel lesson. The week constituted a heavy schedule with the team performances, park outreaches, and teacher training sessions, but we'd been blessed with a last-minute invitation to minister at a ladies' gathering at a small church nearby.

Throughout the week, we had given generously to the schools a large portion of our supplies and gifts. We all felt that this meeting was a special assignment and were sensing to bring a small gift bag for each lady attending. Amazingly, amongst us we had thirty available empty gift bags. Spreading the bags out across the dining table, we set to work. We separated our individually wrapped specialty tea bags, used up the remaining granola bars from our lunches, added some pens, a few extra New Testaments, some bags of pretzels, and anything new from our personal belongings. Each of us, including the guys, gave all we had, but the bags still looked seriously "ungiftable." That night we prayed and worshipped together, overshadowed by the meagre gift bags with negligible contents. We prayed, believing that God would provide everything that heaven had planned.

Arriving home the next day, sweaty and exhausted, we made a race for the showers. My husband noticed two guests arriving in a taxi, and he invited them in. We were speechless! It was Wendy and Jeff Hagar from Burlington, Ontario. What were they doing here? What were the chances? Wendy, the founder and director of Sew on Fire, a ministry to missions, had filled our suitcases with wonderful school supplies before we had left. Jeff and Wendy were in St. Lucia on vacation and had come to check out our mission! What a joy!

Their visit would have been encouragement enough, but Wendy shared how God had directed her to pack an extra suitcase in faith, not knowing why or whether they would be able to arrange a rendezvous with us. When Wendy opened that suitcase, we didn't know whether to cry, scream, or hug her to pieces! It was stuffed to capacity with beautiful silk scarves, necklaces, journals, filled cosmetic bags, and personal care items. Ninety per cent of the items were specifically for women! We had presented our limited and humble offering to the Lord, and He had multiplied it to "full and overflowing!" Who can ever imagine the ways of our God?

The team learned a valuable and enduring lesson that day. Give what you have, give from the heart, give generously, and give in faith, believing God will do what only He can do. Loaves and fishes in His hand had filled multiple buckets with food. Tea bags, pens, and pretzels in His hand had now multiplied to fill thirty bags with silk scarves, personal care items, and lots of love!

Faith was stirred on the team, and women at the church were touched by the power of God. His presence was tangible. Hearts were healed, and love was poured out in generous portions. "Faith is taking the first step even when you don't see the whole staircase."[7]

Lord, let my offerings be ones of faith, given from the heart. Heaven's multiplication is so exciting! Multiply the effectiveness of all that I give to you. In Jesus' name.

---

7 "Martin Luther King, Jr.," AZQuotes, https://www.azquotes.com/quote/158971?ref=faith, accessed June 29, 2021.

Faith Fastened to His Promise

Day Nineteen

"Now faith brings our hopes into reality and becomes the foundation needed to acquire the things we long for. It is all the evidence required to prove what is still unseen."

—Hebrews 11:1, TPT

Her barrenness was not only a matter of regret, but it was a reproach. She was a woman of sorrowful spirit. Her infertility confined her to a place of social embarrassment and loneliness. On top of that, she shared her husband with Peninnah, a woman of ample fertility who ridiculed her with jeers and hurtful words. Hannah's story, recorded in 1 Samuel 1 and 2, is a story of courage and faith in the midst of pain and mockery. She was loved by her husband, Elkanah, but even his encouragement and favour couldn't comfort her. Peninnah's demeaning words eroded Hannah's self-confidence, and her heart was torn because of childlessness.

Year after year, as they went up to the house of the Lord to bring their sacrifice, Peninnah would provoke Hannah, and on this particular visit, Hannah's emotions erupted into tears. She wept until she couldn't even eat. When Eli, the priest, reprimanded her for appearing drunk during the festival of sacrifice, this additional judgement must have been unbearable. She confessed to Eli that she was pouring her soul out to the Lord, recognizing afresh that her relief was in God alone. The scripture doesn't mention that Hannah shared details of her prayer with Eli, but she was praying in faith for a son. She vowed that if God would answer her prayer, she would give the child to

Him to be His servant in the temple. Eli prophesied to her: *"Go in peace and the God of Israel grant your petition ..."* (1 Samuel 1:17, NKJV).

Hannah had great respect for Eli as a priest of the Lord, and when she heard his words, faith rose in her. She believed and fastened her faith to God's promise (1 Samuel 1:18–20). She could move beyond the oppression of her pain—she was no longer downcast. Something transforming happened in her heart in those moments. Her fractured but persistent faith was fanned with fresh hope and vision, and she knew that her always faithful God was at work. Her response was worship. She left, believing in His power to do great things, even though nothing had changed in the natural. She saw the promise, by faith, and gave thanks! We know that God not only answered Hannah's prayer but later blessed her with three more sons and two daughters.

Our pain and brokenness don't have the final word. Part of God's bigger plan for Elkanah and Hannah was the timing of their son's birth. Samuel needed to be born at a crucial time in history. Not sooner. Not later. God took the waiting time to strengthen and prepare Hannah's heart to become a mother who would be willing to allow her son to be brought up by Eli and raised as a priest. God had a plan that needed Samuel at the right place, at the right time, throughout his years.

God hears and answers the prayers of those who come to Him in faith, who fasten their faith to His promise. If you have a promise from God for the salvation of a loved one, a breakthrough in a relationship, a long-awaited change in financial security—don't stop praying and don't stop believing! Despite the disappointment and pain you may face while you wait, God is faithful. When the answer is different than expected, continue to trust His heart and His plan. Choose to worship and walk in a faith that always brings pleasure to His heart.

Father God, when pain and brokenness attempt to close a chapter of my story, help me to remember that they do not have the final word. When I can't see your bigger plan, help me to trust in your faithfulness and goodness as you unfold my destiny and your victory in my life.

Faith Tested

Day Twenty

Contributed by Penny Lane

"See, I have refined you, but not like silver; I have tested you in the furnace of adversity."

—Isaiah 48:10, NRSV

Our faith is strengthened and deepened by the tests and trials of life. However painful and contrary to our natural thinking, from God's perspective, trials serve to better us. John Maxwell says, "A faith that cannot be tested cannot be trusted."[8]

One of my favourite Bible passages is the book of Esther. I love how her faith and obedience brought deliverance to the whole nation of Israel. Esther made the choice that whatever the cost, she would obey God's plan: *"I will go to the king… and if I perish, I perish"* (Esther 4:16b, NRSV).

It's easy to have strong faith when all is going well! But when we've reached the end of our own resources, that's when we discover what's really deep inside of us, or perhaps what is lacking, in the faith department. A first confrontation with what I had always believed to be a strong faith in my personal walk with God proved to be a testing of an unexpected proportion, and one that revealed a shocking and disturbing lack. Why? Because my faith had never really been tested, and I had wrongly assumed that it was building muscle without exercise!

My husband and I, along with our two young children, spent four years in Northern Canada in mission work with a precious First Nations

---

8 "A Faith that Cannot Be Tested Cannot Be Trusted," Sami Cone, https://www.samicone.com/faith-cannot-be-tested-cannot-be-trusted/, accessed July 30, 2021.

community. I found myself in a new culture, far away from the comfort of home, family, and friends. Though homesick and lonely, I was trying to adjust. Feeling insecure, ill-equipped, and vulnerable, I felt my identity and role as a young wife and mother being challenged. Living in a very close-knit community with other leaders meant relationships were often strained and difficult.

Like Esther, I had decisions to make that included taking a risk trusting God for the right outcome. OK, it wasn't a life and death situation like Esther's, and it wouldn't have the potential to take down an entire nation, but it seemed like that size of a mountain to me! The options were traumatic and life changing at the time.

Holy Spirit used this situation to reveal my need for dependence on Him. I admit I didn't appreciate it at the time. I probably prayed more than a few prayers, asking for a way out and telling God He could do more. I had to wrestle through the "whys" and the disappointment. But hindsight is always welcomed in our walk with God. As I look back, I'm thankful for that crisis of faith. It has brought me to a place of strength, confidence, and faith that I wouldn't have reached otherwise. I can embrace new challenges with a deep trust in a God who is transforming me for His purposes and one who has a bigger Kingdom plan of which I get to be a part.

Wherever you find yourself, whatever your current situation, perhaps like Esther you've come to the Kingdom *"for such a time as this"* (Esther 4:14). It may be that God will ask you to do something that can only be done by faith in Him. God doesn't waste opportunities. "Great faith is the product of great fights. Great testimonies are the outcome of great tests. Great triumphs can only come out of great trials."[9]

Father God, I am reminded that Esther counted the cost and chose to obey. I'm choosing, in your strength, to cultivate faith and trust you, even in the difficult opportunities.

---

9   "Smith Wigglesworth," AZQuotes, https://www.azquotes.com/quote/491763?ref=test-of-faith, accessed July 30, 2021.

The Heart of Worship

Day Twenty-One

By faith Abel presented to God a sacrifice more acceptable than his brother Cain's. By faith Abel learned he was righteous, as God Himself testified by approving his offering. And by faith he still speaks, although his voice was silenced by death.

—Hebrews 11:4, VOICE (emphasis added)

Unlike his parents, Adam and Eve, Abel didn't get to live in a perfect environment and see God face-to-face. However, you can guarantee that he and his brother, Cain, heard lots about those walks in the evening, the taste of the fruit, the peace, and the beauty. You can be sure they heard about the consequences of sin and disobedience, and how much their parents gave up for a moment of curiosity and deception. Although we're not clear on the established spiritual laws at the time, we know that Adam and Eve would have been imparting to their sons an understanding of the prescribed ways of worship.

Cain and Abel were the first of many feuding siblings. In Genesis 4, we observe their time of worship. Cain, the oldest son, was a tiller of the ground, growing vegetables and fruit. Abel, the younger, was the one who raised the flocks. When it was time to bring an offering of sacrifice, Cain gathered some of the produce he had grown and brought it to offer to the Lord. Abel, on the other hand, brought both the first and the best of his flock and their fat. The contrast isn't between an offering of plant life and an offering of animal life, but between an easy offering, meant to fulfill an obligation, and a generous offering prompted by a believing heart. It was about how the offering was made. Motivation and heart attitude are all-important. God looked with favour on Abel and his offering because of Abel's faith. The offering was made by one who believed God and believed who He was. He offered it in obedience and humility, recognizing the need to address his own sin with the blood sacrifice. Cain, it appears, was going through the motions but didn't see himself in light of a perfect God.

There's a difference between worshipping God the way we want to and the way He wants us to. To come into His presence, we must always deal with our sin, and God sees the seriousness that we display in believing who He is. The worshipper and his offering are inseparable (1 Corinthians 6:17). Because God couldn't accept Cain's offering, neither could He accept him. God, in compassion, gave Cain an opportunity to turn things around, but his anger and jealousy led to him murdering his brother, Abel. Abel, however, is remembered as a champion of faith because of his better sacrifice (Hebrews 11). The scriptures say that through a more excellent sacrifice, Abel obtained witness that he was righteous and that through his offering, he still speaks to us today. Faith is believing, but it's even more. It's living in a way that shows your trust in God. The Lord treasures faith that rests in obedience.

Worship is our response to God, expressed in the things we think, say, and do. Abel's testimony of worship still speaks. It reminds us that the attitude of our hearts is of utmost importance. Faith says we truly believe who God is and that we aren't willing to cut corners on what He deserves. Faith says we will worship with a heart of love and not just out of obligation. Faith says obedience matters. Faith says we will recognize our unworthiness and His perfection. Yes, Abel's life still speaks to us today. What is it speaking to you?

Holy Spirit, search my heart. May I always be ready to give my first and my best. My obedience matters to you. Let my life be a testimony to my trust in you.

Faith Discovered

Day Twenty-Two

Contributed by Betty Chisholm

"I have been crucified with Christ; and it is no longer I who live, but Christ lives in me; and the life which I now live in the flesh I live by faith in the Son of God, who loved me and gave Himself up for me."

—Galatians 2:20, NASB

I could hardly believe the visibility I was gaining in the music industry—performance opportunities were plentiful. A letter in the mail invited me to the Canadian Country Music Awards. I found myself looking at the words "Top Female Performance—Country Artist of the Year" and feeling bewildered and empty. Even this recognition of popularity and success in my music career wasn't satisfying my longing heart.

After not being selected as the winner, I began a slow journey into depression. My boys would come home from school to a mom who was hidden away in a dark room with blinds closed and no sign of engagement. I was on grief overload after my dad's death and was inconsolable. With the mental and emotional turmoil, my body went down to ninety-two pounds. I suffered with peptic ulcers, gout, bad circulation, and hair loss. The hopelessness was paralyzing. Prescription medication wreaked havoc on my internal system. Suicidal thoughts came frequently. A therapist was enlisted for support.

The missing ingredient for me, though I didn't know it, was a relationship with Jesus. Looking to the sky one day, I asked with anger, "Is there really a God? If I'm supposed to have faith, how do I get it? Wouldn't my family be better off without me?"

God heard me, and He was at the ready! From Christian books gifted to me, to a gospel tract, to an extended family member who got me to church, He led me on a journey of finding faith. With the encouragement and faith-filled prayers of those people at the church and the study of my Bible, along with my hunger to find Him, something amazing happened! I asked my heavenly Father's forgiveness, invited Him to walk with me, hold me, and heal me. I was truly born again! I began to use every opportunity to learn more.

At my therapy appointment three months later, my faith was exploding! The therapist wondered whether I was living in a fantasy or experiencing a bad drug trip. But the medical reports didn't lie—ulcers gone, gout cleared, thinking clear. Shaking his head, he affirmed that he saw no reason to continue my sessions. As he ushered me to the door, he paused. What came next was hard to believe. Would I be willing to return to his office and share my success with some other patients in similar situations? For this passionate new believer, that offer was better than a year's worth of hot waffles or chocolate cake!

For the next few months, I occupied his main floor on Wednesday afternoons, surrounded by people ready to hear how Jesus could change their lives. The medical staff were astounded with the results! God used my meagre offering of faith to bring life to others ... before I could even pronounce Philippians!

Every day of my faith journey has been an exciting adventure—inside prisons, music ministry, on the streets, and across nations. God has seen me through serious blood clots, surgeries, cancer, and Covid. I know that Christ lives in me. My faith is flourishing, my eyes are fixed on Him, and I know anything is possible to those who believe.

Jesus, thank you for meeting me when I stood needing you, but questioning and hesitant. Thank you for the work of the cross that provides for my salvation, my healing, and my freedom. Keep me ready to boldly share your goodness and your love.

When Faith Builds the House: Part One

Day Twenty-Three

Contributed by Beulah and Howard Courtney

"Therefore everyone who hears these words of mine and puts them into practice is like a wise man who built his house on the rock. The rain came down, the streams rose, and the winds blew and beat against that house; yet it did not fall, because it had its foundation on the rock."

—Matthew 7:24–25

Beulah's Story

I faced the biggest faith challenge of my life in 1985. That was the year my then thirty-five-year-old husband, Bruce, was diagnosed with CML (Chronic Myelogenous Leukemia), discovered during a routine blood test. To say we were shocked with the diagnosis was an understatement. The doctor delivered the grim prognosis: with the proper treatment, maybe he would have two years. Up to this point, Bruce had been a healthy, six-foot-two man who manoeuvred the big transit buses, streetcars, and subways around the city. He loved his job; he loved hunting and fishing. He loved his family, and he loved life!

Bruce and I both served the Lord and had rededicated our lives in 1972. Bruce was a faith giant, much farther ahead in his faith walk than I. He studied the Bible in depth daily. At night he would fall asleep with recorded scriptures playing in his ears. On Saturday mornings, I would smell the coffee, and he'd come and get me to study alongside him. He'd say, "Beulah, you have to build your own faith, and I'll help you do that." That's how my faith began to grow!

Little did I know how much I would need, and lean on, those promises of scripture in the days ahead. Our church family and friends were praying hard for a miracle. At the time of diagnosis, our daughter was eighteen, and our son was ten. They never heard him complain. Bruce would always say he was fine, even when he wasn't. He didn't want them to worry.

God was gracious. He gave us an additional four years beyond the expected two. Some days were challenging, and some were normal, with opportunities to make special memories. On August 15, 1991, at the age of forty-one, Bruce was called home. Written on his memorial stone are these words, "Having walked by faith, he pleased God" (Hebrews 11:5).

My world as I knew it was no more. I'd lost the love of my life. I now had a choice to make: to stay in my grief, or to move forward in the faith walk in which Bruce had discipled me. I didn't deny the pain, but as I allowed God to comfort and encourage me, I also put my faith in Him to the test. I discovered my faith was strong; my trust was in God, and He didn't fail me.

I held an executive administrative position at my workplace and was surrounded by dignitaries and high-level officers. At the celebration of Bruce's life, they, along with a full busload of Bruce's colleagues from the transit commission, heard about the love and power of God, some for the first time. They couldn't understand the strength that was evident in me—*God's strength*. He was the one who carried me, and in the days that followed, He gave me many opportunities to share *"the reason for the hope"* that was within me (1 Peter 3:15). God looked after my children, Sherri and Jason, who both love Jesus today.

For the next eight years, I remained a content widow, serving God with passion and a grateful heart, using every opportunity to share my faith and encourage others in their unique storms. Then, much to my surprise (but not to God's), Heaven sent something totally unexpected my way ... *Read tomorrow's devotional for "the rest of the story!"*

Father, thank you for your strength and comfort in our times of loss. Thank you for those who encourage us in our faith journey with you. May I be faithful to do the same for others.

When Faith Builds the House: Part Two

Day Twenty-Four
Contributed by Beulah and Howard Courtney

"But even if he doesn't. . .

—Daniel 3:18a, NLT

Beulah continues ...

A nd ... that surprise I mentioned in yesterday's devotional? God brought a widower into my life, a pastor who had lost his wife to cancer. An amazing blend was about to take place. My house stood firm, because it was founded upon a rock. Hallelujah! And now for *his* story...

Howard's Story

The news came to us as such a shock. Inside of her was a cancerous tumor the size of a midterm baby, totally undetected until now. Carol and I had always been faith-filled believers. People around us and from unexpected places far away joined with us to express faith for a miracle. Apart from God's intervention, there was little hope. But we agreed that we would travel the road accessing the best available medical procedures along with the best spiritual disciplines.

The challenge for me came with our two teenage boys, Caleb and Gideon. Close friends and loving supportive people told them emphatically that God was going to heal their mother. Though we were believing for that, I needed to know that their faith was bigger than this one miracle. They needed to experience a faith in God that would be stronger and more durable than the miracle of deliverance for their mother. They needed a faith for the "if nots" in life. So we sat down together to vocalize it with them. For the three Hebrew children facing their fiery trial, faith was perfectly evident when they said, "*Our God is able to deliver us,* but if not ..." (Daniel 3:17, 18, NKJV, emphasis added). Faith is not faith when it's seen. Faith is the substance of things hoped for (Hebrews 11:1). *Faith in God is bigger than miracles alone.*

In the end, though, death took her sooner than we wished. The faith of our two boys ... our faith ... not only survived but thrived. Faith is the victory that overcomes the world and all its painful life experiences (1 John 5:4). Even Jesus in His own death saw faith rise from the ashes and life go on. Faith doesn't always give us what we want (Matthew 26:39), but faith sustains us on a level that many can't grasp. My boys are now married and serving the Lord.

God sees the big picture, and He had another plan I didn't foresee. It was beautiful and full of His goodness, joy, and grace. He brought Beulah into my life to become my wife. She too had experienced an overcoming faith during the loss of her spouse. I've learned that God has an ear that hears every prayer, He has relief for every sorrow, and a good plan for every tomorrow. Together, we walk in faith (2 Corinthians 5:7), loving, serving, and growing. His goodness is always chasing us down, and our faith continues to thrive (Hebrews 11:6)!

Beulah and Howard .

We've been abundantly blessed. God has been so good to us! Shortly after we were married, we merged our individual testimonies and have had the privilege of sharing our story of God's faithfulness in a number of churches and special events. We have an amazing family blend of four children. Although it seems like only yesterday, those four now have spouses, and they've given us nine grandchildren and, recently, our first great grandchild. To God be the glory, great things He has done!

Lord, thank you for your incredible presence that we experience daily. May our lives be a witness of your faithfulness and joy to those with whom we come in contact. May our conduct, conversation, and character always line up with our testimony. In Jesus' name. Amen.

The Faith of Four Friends

Day Twenty-Five

"But Jesus said to him, '. . . All things are possible for the one who believes.'"
—Mark 9:23, NASB

Every eye in the house was on Jesus that day, and every ear was attuned to His teaching. Teachers of the law had come from every town of Galilee, Judea, and Jerusalem. In this uncommon crowd of theologians, the presence of God was there to heal. Luke records it in this manner:

> *Then behold, men brought on a bed a man who was paralyzed . . . And when they could not find how they might bring him in, because of the crowd, they went up on the housetop and let him down with his bed through the tiling into the midst before Jesus. When He saw their faith, He said to him, "Man, your sins are forgiven you." . . . He said to the man who was paralyzed, "I say to you, arise, take up your bed, and go to your house." Immediately he rose up before them . . . and departed to his own house . . .*
> —Luke 5:18–20, 24, NKJV

For the four friends, getting their paralytic friend to Jesus required both persistence and faith. They had already carried the sick man through the jostling crowd to no avail, so they had to find an alternative access point to get to Jesus. The best option was the roof. Compelled by their love for this man and a confidence in the power of Jesus to heal, they decided to tear apart this stranger's roof, carve out a man-sized hole, and lower the bedridden man into the midst of the crowd.

What sets this miracle apart in Jesus' ministry is that it wasn't the paralytic, who was both forgiven and healed by Jesus, who was the centre of attention, but the four friends who with unwavering resolve brought the man to Jesus. There's no record that they said anything when they broke through to Jesus. It wasn't what Jesus heard that touched His heart but what He saw. Four sweaty men with dirty faces, hungry for a miracle. *"When He saw their faith ..."* (v. 20, emphasis added), He responded to the man's needs. This miracle is all about a persevering faith that recognized the power of His presence and moved His heart.

There are times when faith is stirred by love for someone who needs to get to Jesus—a brother, a sister, a parent, a child. Sometimes staying in faith for others involves heavy lifting and inconvenience. It means facing the seeming impossibilities that might stand in the way. When the obstacles become too great or hope is hindered, are we prepared to press through for the miracle of salvation or healing?

Sometimes we need to multiply faith by inviting others to help us carry the load (Matthew 18:19). Radical faith, on our part, can bring life-changing results in the life of another who may feel hopeless, discouraged, or abandoned. May the Lord give each of us the courage and strength to walk in an unshakeable faith for those around us who need our help to get to Him.

Lord, thank you for the faithful friends who once carried me on their shoulders and in their hearts, despite the obstacles, to get me to you. Stir my heart to be bold in faith to carry others, no matter how weighty or inconvenient the burden. Teach me how to walk with an unwavering resolve fixed on your unlimited love and grace that is ready to change their lives. Amen.

A Faith that Finishes Well

Day Twenty-Six

Contributed by Shirley Godfrey

"Therefore, since we are surrounded by such a great cloud of witnesses let us throw off everything that hinders ... And let us run with perseverance the race marked out for us."

—Hebrews 12:1

After over sixteen years as a Palliative Care Chaplain, my husband, Ralph, had also completed his secondary career of choice—thirteen years of childcare for his grandsons! Now he was *really* retired. A new opportunity for leisure awaited, and we were off to a wonderful vacation with good friends. For fifty years, Ralph had done an hour of power walking as part of his daily routine. But on this vacation, we noticed something was wrong. Once around the walking course on the cruise ship seemed more than he could handle. We knew he wasn't well.

Once home, Ralph and I made our way to the hospital emergency department. While alone and being prepared for admission, he was told news no one ever wants to hear—he had terminal cancer. Ralph was a gentle, humble man of unwavering faith. As he relayed the news to me soon after, it carried a supernatural peace. "I'm in His hands," were the first thoughts expressed.

Although the cancer was stage four, Ralph's amazing oncologist worked with him to devise a variety of treatment plans, always measuring the effectiveness and changing them as needed. Ralph had no sense of denial. He simply wanted to "live" until he died—after all, our only granddaughter was getting married. Her Poppa was her first love, and she was his Sweetie. She asked him to officiate at the wedding. This was after almost one year of routine, every-third-week chemotherapy. The wedding was still more than a year away! Despite my suggestion to her, she didn't move up the date.

As Ralph neared the end of year three, and the good days between chemo sessions were almost nonexistent, he would sit at the breakfast table with his head on his crossed arms and say, "I can't let Desiree down." It was clear that the strength he had for holding on was not his own. His faith saw a finish line that included Desiree's marriage ceremony. I was praying with everything in me and trying hard to believe that he would live to do it.

On the day of the wedding, we prepared at the nearby hotel. Ralph was dressed, with shoes and socks still to go. I knelt in front of him with the socks, ready to pull them over his swollen feet. He'd been unable to wear socks for many weeks. The shoes were slippers with Velcro closing. As I knelt and prayed, a blanket of peace seemed to enfold me. At that moment, I had the assurance that this day would be as hoped. I was calm, so aware that a multitude of friends who had asked the actual time of the service were before God praying for us. Their faith was supporting us. My task was accomplished, and Ralph entered the banquet hall and accompanied the groom to the front of the room.

In one month and one day after the wedding, Ralph told me, in one word, he wanted to go "home." Jesus was waiting, and his request was granted. His faith in an ever-present God provided an uncommon perseverance and resolve to finish well. At every turn, in every treatment session, in every struggle, and while performing that very special wedding, Ralph knew what it meant to have his eyes fixed on the eternal and be "in His hands."

Heavenly Father, I declare that I too am in your hands. You have planned my life, with a hope and a future designed uniquely for me. I'm choosing to live life to the full as you cheer me on!

A Faith Seeded

Day Twenty-Seven
Contributed by Anita Hanna

"My old identity has been co-crucified with Christ and no longer lives. And now the essence of this new life is no longer mine, for the Anointed One lives his life through me—we live in union as one! My new life is empowered by the faith of the Son of God who loves me so much that he gave himself for me, dispensing his life into mine!"

—Galatians 2:20, TPT

I was only two, but I clearly remember the piercing and horrifying sound of the siren, warning us that war was upon us. I recall my mother rushing my two bothers and me to what I later learned was an underground shelter. I remember little else but the darkness. The year was 1990. The place? Baghdad, Iraq. My father was a soldier in an ongoing war between Iraq and Kuwait. By 1995, my parents knew we must leave Iraq and make a temporary home for the family in Jordan.

Memories of Jordan are clear. By the age of eight, my innocence had been stripped from me, and though I hated it, I had no understanding until my early teens of what had happened. While in Jordan, my mother found a Christian private school where my brothers could stay in the dorm and I could attend classes. The principal gave us books with Bible stories in them. I treasured them, and something eternal was seeded into my heart. Though we didn't attend church, my parents understood in their Catholic faith that there was a God, and they would pray for safety. I was sure that their God, if He existed, would hear our prayer to get to Canada. There was a hope and expectation in a God that I didn't know, yet trusted. My parents would declare often, even under threat of having to return to Iraq, that we would soon get our papers.

After three years of struggle, hope, and prayer, we flew to Canada. And the new life began. Low-income housing. Disappointment. Absentee parents working long hours. Anger. Screaming. Triggered memories. Wounded hearts. At Easter and Christmas, we would go to church—Assyrian/Chaldean/Arabic or English, we just went through the motions. I became consumed by this world and began dipping into occult practices. I was empty, lost, and depressed, but I loved "people."

In March of 2018, a colleague at work invited me to church. The morning we were to go, hesitation and nervousness kicked in. Ready to cancel, I heard a voice that said, "Reason with me." That voice reassured me, and a strange peace came over me. Months later, I read Isaiah 1:18a. Wow! That was the voice of God: *"Come now, let us reason together, says the Lord: though your sins are like scarlet, they shall be as white as snow"* (ESV). The church was Catch the Fire in Toronto (airport). Worship began, and I instantly felt the Spirit of God. I burst into unstoppable sobs—an encounter I will never forget. A great hunger began, and I returned every Sunday. I gave my life to Jesus in the women's washroom with the colleague who to this day is a dear sister to me. I was water baptized and attended a powerful week at their School of Ministry.

Most recently, God has led me to Lakemount Worship Centre in Grimsby. Life Groups, Internship, prayer ministry, wise counsel, heart healing, and transformation have all been part of these past three years. There's no doubt that God planted a seed of faith in me as a child. He watched over it, watered it, and protected it. Now I've really learned how to cultivate my faith, and it's growing exponentially. There is a God in heaven who is faithful to His promises and the plans He has for us. Every day, He is truly "dispensing His life into mine!" Praise God!

Jesus, thank you for your endless love that pursues us and protects us as we journey toward your welcoming arms. When my faith is broken, disappointed, or weak, I will trust you to watch over it, bringing restoration and new hope. My heart rejoices in your faithfulness.

A Faith Rewarded

Day Twenty-Eight

"fixing our eyes on Jesus, the pioneer and perfecter of faith . . ."
—Hebrews 12:2a

For eighteen years, her back muscles have been knotted, her vertebrae lacking alignment, and her nerves pinched and piercing. Her back is arched and painful. She doesn't see what others see and take for granted—the beautiful rays of the sunshine dancing behind wispy, white clouds, or the faces of people close by. She's most familiar with the dust and dirt of the streets, the array of shabby sandals, and the tatters on the hems of worn garments.

As Jesus is reading in the synagogue that day, His attention is turned to this bent-over woman. In one glance, every fragment of her life converges—the suffering, the loneliness, the rejection. But above it all, He sees her faith. She has come to worship, in her pain, as she does every Sabbath, knowing she may be pushed aside, scorned, or, at best, ignored.

When Jesus calls her forward, she feels all eyes turn her way. Her twisted body tenses, imagining the glares. She gathers the courage to respond and shuffles toward Him. Altar calls take decisiveness and fortitude, but this one is not for everyone in the crowd. It is a call for her alone. Those few seconds seem like a lifetime, but as He speaks, *"Woman, you are set free from your infirmity,"* (Luke 13:12), her heart begins to race with both wonder and delight.

As Jesus puts His hands on her, her bent-over body immediately responds to His touch, and every part of her being comes to attention. Her eyes of gratitude and joy meet His, her body now erect. After all these years of being diminished in stature, she stands tall. Hands raised and eyes turned toward heaven, she begins to praise the God whom she has come to worship.

The synagogue official is infuriated that the service has been disrupted and the Sabbath dishonoured. This is not on the order of service and certainly doesn't align with the required religious practices and traditions. He and his entourage of supporters, minds fixed on adherence to the rules, miss the beauty of the miracle that is right before their eyes. Jesus is angered that traditions and programs would take priority over a person in need. How dare they treat this daughter of Abraham, who has an equal share in all the blessings of the Abrahamic covenant, in such a manner! He is fierce in His response, as their assessment lacks both compassion and consistency. When Jesus points out their hypocrisy, they are humiliated (Luke 13:15). The crowd, however, is blessed and amazed with what Jesus has just done for the woman.

Sometimes faith is hidden in perseverance and pain. Jesus sees it, even when we don't. Often there are those around us who walk in incredible faith, a persevering faith and a faith that determines to worship in spite of struggle. Some have been believing for their miracle for many years but have set their hearts on Him, not simply on the miracle. They too may have suffered more than physical pain—perhaps loss of social interaction, loss of friends, abandonment, mistreatment, dreams that have died. I wonder if there were any in the crowd that day who had remained in faith, supportive of that woman in her journey to wholeness. Were any seeing in her their answer to prayer—or were they simply onlookers?

When others are bent low, confined, restricted, in need of a touch from Jesus, we have been afforded the wonderful invitation to walk with them. It's not our part to determine His timing or response but simply to believe with them in faith. If they can persevere, then so can we, and we can do it with love, trusting a God of compassion to see them, touch them, and cause them, by His power, to stand tall.

Jesus, may I be more than an onlooker to the needs of others. Help me to exercise my faith on their behalf in prayer and practical support. May I not become weary in doing good but rather be refreshed by the joy of seeing the bent-over ones stand tall and whole by your power.

Faith in Uncertainty

Day Twenty-Nine

"God is the one who began this good work in you, and I am certain that he won't stop before it is complete..."

—Philippians 1:6, CEV

After having taught school for just over thirty years, I sensed the Lord had something new and exciting in mind, even though I had always loved this career, the kids, and the great staff members who became friends. As I drove through Hamilton one summer afternoon, I passed the Crossroads Christian Communication Centre and felt a heavy tug on my heart that I was to volunteer. But with a full-time job, family, foster children, and all my church commitments, there was no time for an additional assignment. It would involve a reduction in my teaching time, and with retirement just around the corner, it made no sense. My pension would be significantly affected, as it was based on the five most recent years of teaching. I was in the land of "maybe."

I was reminded of 1 Samuel 14:1–14, where Jonathan sensed he should cross over to the Philistine outpost, but he was uncertain whether it was the plan of God. After the inner struggle, he talked to his armour-bearer and suggested, *"Come, let's go over... Perhaps the Lord will act in our behalf. Nothing can hinder the Lord from saving, whether by many or by few"* (v. 6, emphasis added). His armour-bearer affirmed the decision saying, *"...Go ahead; I am with you heart and soul"* (v. 7b). They agreed upon a plan to watch for God's confirmation on their approach, and they saw a great victory. They were uncertain of what to do, but they knew their God!

Then there was Jehoshaphat (2 Chronicles 20), who had received a report that a vast coalition army was coming against Judah to wipe them out. He inquired of the Lord, and in the place of uncertainty, openly confessed that he had no battle plan, no strategy. His faith rested on God's everlasting faithfulness to His people, and he prayed, *"We do not know what to do, but our eyes are on you"* (V. 12b).

When making decisions, we ask, "How do I know this is God? How do I know if I should take this risk?" Our eyes must always be on Him. Jehoshaphat called the nation to prayer and fasting—a great choice! An additional ingredient in Jonathan's situation was choosing to talk to the right person. Sometimes we need someone to help us weigh our uncertainty against the "whole" Word of God and respond to our "maybe" with wisdom and honesty.

I knew I couldn't sit in fear and uncertainty for long, but it takes faith to move on a "maybe." I decided to pray, talk to the right person(s), and move forward. I knew I could trust God's promise that even if I slipped, He'd be there. I reduced my teaching time for the next three years, which allowed me to volunteer on the prayer lines and prepare and film a prayer training course for Crossroad's prayer partners across Canada. It gave me time to step into retirement, accept a position on pastoral staff at a church, complete some religious studies, and move through to ordination. Those opportunities were far beyond what I saw, but I was able to look beyond the temporal and exercise faith in a good God in the process.

"The miracle is often in the "maybe.'"[10] Faith sometimes requires that we step out of the boat of familiarity, with eyes focused on Him. I have found that faith, when aligned with the Word of God, passes the test in times of uncertainty. As we learn to recognize His voice and how He works in us, we can wholeheartedly trust His tugs.

O Lord, when I face uncertainty, be magnified in my eyes. Help me to walk in both wisdom and faith, with a heart that lives out obedience.

---

10 Redefined TV, "Faith Requires Taking a Risk," YouTube video, 4:27, June 12, 2020.

Finding the Way to Him

Day Thirty

"Have courage! Get up! Jesus is calling for you!"

—Mark 10:49b, TPT

He was blind (Mark 10:46–52). People made a lot of assumptions about him as they passed him by each day. Some believed he deserved his blindness—it was God's judgement on him for sin. Some were sure it was his parents who had done wrong. He was worthless, helpless, and, with nothing to give, he was a drain on society. Begging was the only thing he could do to survive. People didn't even take the time to find out his name. He was only known as the son of Timaeus. Bar–Timaeus, a crumpled-up beggar on the side of the road, left behind in his private pain, hearing the cruel comments of "despicable" and "useless."

He hears trickles of conversation on this particular day that Jesus the Nazarene will be passing by. Bartimaeus feels he almost "knows" Him from the many fragments of stories he's heard from the passersby. Not long ago he overheard them saying that He was the one spoken of in Isaiah who would be a light to the Gentiles, to open eyes that are blind, and release from their dungeons those who sit in darkness. Now He's going to be travelling by!

He sits in his thoughts, stirred with possibility and hope, and determines he must not miss this opportunity. He begins to shout from the side of the road: "Jesus, son of David, have mercy on me." Many from the crowd try to quiet him and keep him in his place, but Bartimaeus re-doubles his efforts. He begins to shout louder: "Son of David, have mercy on me."

When Jesus hears him, He stops and speaks to those nearby, instructing them to call him to come to Him. Bartimaeus jumps to his feet, casting his cloak aside. He leaves it with no intention of returning to it. His faith speaks that a new identity is imminent. He can hear the whispers of contempt, but desperate people don't let a crowd keep them from Jesus.

Jesus asks him, "What do you want me to do for you?" Without hesitation, Bartimaeus answers, "Rabbi, I want to see." In his mind, the hurricane of thoughts whirl about. *I want to be out of this prison. I want to see. I want to be able to run the streets of Jericho.* Jesus not only hears what he asks, but He sees into the tempest of his mind. Bartimaeus is beginning to get a vision of the new man he will be. Jesus says, "Your faith has made you whole." In that moment, Bartimaeus comes from darkness into light. As sunshine floods his eyes, he turns from the crowd to see the eyes of Jesus. Such tenderness and love he has never experienced.

What faith for a blind man! Enough faith to risk a bold and desperate cry into a disinterested and condescending crowd. Enough faith to ask for what was, in the natural, impossible. Enough faith to believe that this was truly the one spoken of by the prophet Isaiah. Enough faith to leave behind the only identity he had known.

Jesus asked for a blind man to find his way to Him! Now He is calling you! He calls:

The blind to see.
The deaf to hear.
The guilty to be pardoned.
The empty to be filled.
The weary to find rest.
The grieving to be comforted.
The weak to become strong.

It may stretch your faith, but do what you need to do to get to Him.

Jesus, I'm hearing your call. Take me past the disinterested and the condescending. I want to live out a life of faith, declaring you are the only answer, and you matter most.

Small Group Helps

This devotional journey welcomes the participation of others in a small group setting, either in person or online. Each participant will need their own copy of the book and can journal any take-aways or questions from their daily readings. In a small group setting, all participants should be reading the devotional entries at the same time so that discussions centre around the same readings on any given week. Discussing your insights will reveal some impacting and exciting truths. By having the group read one extra entry on week three and week four, you can complete the journey in the four weeks. An alternative is to read six per week, taking Sundays off and making it a five-week journey.

The group leader may select two to five questions from the following list for the weekly group meeting, which should run between sixty and seventy minutes. Vary your selection of questions from the list, adapting them to your group's focus. Be sure to allow time for personal thoughts, testimonies of growth, and any questions. Keep a scriptural view as foundational and expect God to meet with you as you gather. The preferred leadership style for this topic is facilitation, where the leader encourages both participation and time boundaries during sharing. The facilitator should be familiar with the material and keep the discussion moving.

Discussion Questions (Choose your own adventure!)

General Questions for any week: Numbers 1–6

1. Which biblical character or event was most impactful to your growth this week?
2. What life lesson did you learn from that character or event?
3. Which testimony stood out for you this week? Share what you gained from it.
4. Share one truth from this week's readings that might be relevant to pass along to a specific friend for discussion in the future.
5. Choose a scripture verse from this week's devotionals and unpack what it means in your life right now.
6. Talk about your greatest faith challenge right now and pray for one another.

Questions specific to particular readings: Numbers 7–33

7. When the woman touched the hem of His garment, why was it important to Jesus that she not just disappear in the crowd?
8. Have you ever reached out after a long struggle and had a miracle? Share with your group.
9. We've all had some faith wrestles. Share one of yours. How do you see God working in the wrestle?
10. How are you allowing your faith to work in God's invitation to others? What is difficult in sharing your faith?
11. Like Hannah, when the answer is different than expected, do you continue to trust His heart and His plan? Explain.
12. Has brokenness ever attempted to close a chapter of your story? Explain.
13. If it wasn't a cake, what was one of the most personal desires of your heart that you have believed God for against all odds? Share your story.
14. How are you living your life to leave a legacy of faith?

15. Are there any individuals in your life who have shared a legacy of faith with you? Share how they have done that.

16. Have you ever found yourself in a climate of pressure, rejection, or loneliness like Noah? How did it test your faith?

17. How do you think Grandma Dinnick developed an unwavering faith that allowed her to go back to sleep when her husband still wasn't home?

18. What do you think God was doing when Heide and Carl were each pressing into Him?

19. God often delivers us from having to face the furnace, but sometimes He delivers us in the furnace. Has this been your experience? Explain.

20. How important is timing in seeing victory? (Consider Amie and Ken's story or your own.)

21. How can you apply "seeing differently" like Joshua and Caleb to your own Christian walk?

22. Are you fighting in prayer for someone like Joe's mother did? Share with the group and pray for one another.

23. Is there a time recently where Jesus stepped into your boat?

24. What are some factors that made the centurion's faith amazing?

25. Penny knew that if she wanted to grow in her walk with God, it would mean taking a risk. What would you have done and why?

26. Talk about Smith Wigglesworth's words from Day Twenty: "Great faith is the product of great fights. Great testimonies are the outcome of great tests. Great triumphs can only come out of great trials."

27. How does Howard and Beulah's story speak to you?

28. Sometimes staying in faith for others involves heavy lifting and inconvenience. How are you doing with the inconveniences?

29. Take a few minutes to share with your group the names of some faithful friends who once carried you on their shoulders.

30. How does the bent-over woman's courage and faith speak to you?

31. Have you faced uncertainty? How do you walk in faith through uncertainty?

32. Bartimaeus jumped to his feet, casting his cloak aside. He left it with no intention of returning to it. His faith spoke a new identity that was imminent. How important is it for us to cast our cloak aside as we walk in faith?

33. If Jesus came by this group today and you heard Him calling you, why would He be calling?

Note: As a bonus, for the first eighteen months after release, contact the author at ruth.teakle@gmail.com to have one of the contributors as a guest (online only) at one of your group sessions. Details upon request.

Contributors

Dr. Dayo Adeyemo, PhD., P.Eng., FNICE., MNSE., MBA is a civil engineer by training and a pastor by calling. Presently, he is the pastor of RCCG Royal House St. Catharines, where he serves with his wife, Pastor Ola. They are blessed with two children, Daniel and Esther. Prior to moving to Canada in 2001, he pastored in Nigeria.

Pastor Dayo is a licensed professional engineer in Ontario, where he currently practises as a civil/geotechnical engineering consultant in a leading Canadian consulting firm. He has practised professional engineering in Africa, Europe, and North America. He's also a licensed General Practice Psychotherapist (G.P.P) and has received two honorary doctorate degrees from Canadian seminaries.

The prophetic mandate on his life is to raise up a people of power and purpose with passion for Jesus. Pastor Dayo has a strong healing anointing on his life and hosts an annual revival meeting, "God of Wonders." He has authored several books, including *Walking in Your Prophetic Destiny, I will Reach my Goal, Discerning the Will of God,* and *The God that Speaks.*

RCCG Royal House:
https://www.youtube.com/channel/UCIWyX8BTo50l9qQ85set3Pw.

Shirley Brown and her (late) husband, Ross, were married in 1955 and raised their four children in the Toronto/ Newmarket area of Ontario. Shirley is an author and inspirational speaker who has shared her journey on both radio and television across Canada as well as in the Canadian *Reader's Digest* and numerous Christian magazines. Her writings include *A Walk through God's Word* ladies' Bible study and her book, *Vanished: What Happened to My Son?* (available on Amazon.ca). For twelve years Shirley gave oversight to the organization "Courage to Cope," which she founded to assist families with missing children. Shirley speaks and writes with authenticity, vulnerability, and grace. At eighty-five, she continues to serve the body of Christ through prayer ministry at her home church, The River International, in Ancaster, Ontario.

Born as number five in a family of seven children, Betty Chisholm has always been curious and adventurous. As a pre-schooler, an early fascination with fire left her tottering between life and death. Having journeyed through a lifetime of medical interventions, shame, abortion, and a broken marriage, Betty stands as a trophy of God's grace, healing, and redemptive plan. She's an ordained minister with Open Bible Faith Fellowship (OBFF) and has served as founder and director of Prison Revival Ministries for thirty-five years. Her ministry has included Music with a Mission, a local Aglow presidency, international missions, speaking and teaching engagements, and media interviews. She has written her story in book form, titled *Out of the Flame*. As wife to John, mother, grandmother, and retired career hairdresser, Betty's prayer is that her transparency in relating her journey to victory will bring hope and freedom to others. Betty and John reside in St. Catharines, Ontario.

Beulah (Collins) Courtney was born in Hare Bay, Newfoundland, and Howard Courtney was born in Orangeville, Ontario. Following graduation, Beulah moved to Ontario to work and spent most of her very successful career as an executive administrator with Nortel. During that time, her husband, Bruce Luscombe, lost his courageous battle with leukemia. Howard Courtney, following graduation, attended Bible college and entered the ministry with the PAOC. While he was serving as lead pastor in Innisfil Community Church, his wife, Carol Hogeboom, succumbed to her battle with cancer following a tenacious and heroic fight. God had a plan. He brought Beulah and Howard together, and they serve the congregation in Innisfil and lead the church in the operation of the Innisfil Food Bank. Howard has been a volunteer with the Canadian Red Cross for over fifty years, most recently in Disaster Services. Beulah's joy involves giving oversight to the development and growth of The Clothing Depot, located at the church, which recycles good used clothing free to local residents. Both Beulah and Howard are recipients of Canadian medals for volunteer service in the community. In their seldom found spare time, they like to travel, take long walks, spend time with family, and shop.

www.innisfilchurch.com

Joe Courtney was born and raised in Orangeville, Ontario. He married his wife, Sandra, in 1970. He's had a career as a paramedic, and over the last number of years as an auctioneer. He can work the bidding at any auction with words that roll off the tongue at record speeds and could give Christie's or Sotheby's some good competition. Joe's retirement hours are spent at his Courtney Auctions warehouse in Listowel, Ontario and serving in his home church, Crossroads Life Church, in Harriston. Joe's heart for evangelism has sought out the broken and lost, and he has led many to freedom in Christ.

www.courtneyauctions.ca

Shirley Godfrey (BA, BSW, MSW) and her late husband, Ralph, were married in Brantford, Ontario in 1965. Both, at that time, were officers/pastors in the Salvation Army, Ralph having served for ten years and Shirley for two. Throughout their officership, they were blessed with varying appointments in Ontario, Bermuda, Nova Scotia, and Manitoba. They returned to Toronto, where Ralph became Director of Pastoral Care at Toronto Grace Hospital for over sixteen years. During this time, Shirley served as a chaplain at Toronto Grace Hospital and Scarborough Grace Hospital, returning to Toronto Grace as a social worker after completing her social work degrees.

Following retirement, Shirley continued part time at Mount Sinai Hospital. For ten years, she volunteered as a group facilitator at her Corps/church in English conversation classes. These connections have provided rich relationships with many, some who have now resettled across the globe. Shirley loves to make muffins, sip a cup of good coffee with a friend, entertain, read, or spend time with family.

Judy Hampton lives in Smithville in the heart of the Niagara Region with her husband, Wayne, and Havanese pup, Benita. She attended Niagara College in the 1970s for Dental Assisting and worked in that field for twenty-two years. She then began working with her husband in their business of selling pre-owned vehicles. She obtained a Bachelor of Practical Ministry degree from Wagner Leadership Institute and has attended Eastern Pentecostal Bible College.

Judy has been actively involved in many ministry areas, including work with single parent families, short term missions, Life Groups, and prayer ministry, as well as serving as a ministry elder at her church, Lakemount Worship Centre. Her great joy is to share the life-changing, redeeming love of Jesus with people anywhere God leads. She's always up for a new travel adventure and enjoys choral music, cooking, gardening, and a dark roast coffee, especially if it involves catching up with a friend. She enjoys spending quality time with extended family and finds cruising in their convertible or classic car with Wayne a great way to de-stress!

Anita Hanna was born in Baghdad, Iraq and lived in Jordan for three years. She immigrated to Canada with her family in 1998. Since graduation, she has enjoyed a successful career in administration. Her joy in ministry is loving people and seeing people come to know and receive Jesus Christ as their Lord and Saviour. As God has moved so powerfully in transforming her life, she believes that God can do the same for others. She loves to read, go for runs, do the stairs, and spend time with family. Anita is currently employed at Lakemount Worship Centre as the Executive Assistant to the Lead Pastor.

www.lakemount.ca

Penny Lane was born in Welland, Ontario and was sibling to two older and two younger brothers. She's been married to her high school sweetheart, Keith, for forty-eight years, and they have two children and seven grandchildren. Penny has enjoyed a full slate of ministry activities, including Northern Canada First Nations, pastor with Catch the Fire, and intercessor on the Canadian Fire Wall. She's also had a successful real estate career in Niagara for fifteen years. While Penny loves nature walks and hospitality, you'll find her currently living her life of ease and freedom full-time in a fifth wheeler alongside her husband. They are traversing Canada and the US, stopping for welcomed visits with family and friends along the way. She continues to be passionate about God's presence and ready to help others recognize and walk out their destinies.

As the President of Bible League Canada (BLC), Paul Richardson leads a team of Canadians that resource and equip Christians in more than forty nations to reach their people with the living Word of God. Through his work with BLC, Paul's extensive travels give him a front row seat for some of God's activity around the globe. Prior to leading BLC, Paul spent twenty years pastoring in Ontario churches—from a small, rural church plant to a 3,500-member congregation in a large urban centre, with a multi-staff team.

With his enthusiasm for God's Word, love for people from all nations, and demonstrated willingness to take risks that require faith, Paul is an inspiring speaker. "My prime goal in life is not to be comfortable but to do what it takes to see the Kingdom of God advanced," says Paul.

Paul and his wife, Dale, have four grown sons, one grandchild, and two well-loved Shih Tzu's.

www.bibleleague.ca

While Catherine (Cathy) Ritson's childhood years were spent in Simcoe, Ontario, her marriage to Ken took her to Niagara Falls, where they resided for fourteen years while raising their three children. Cathy's career path involved sales, executive secretarial positions, and retail consulting prior to a move to Toronto, where she and Ken entered the Salvation Army Training College to become officers (pastors). For thirty-three years they served across Canada, pastoring churches, overseeing public relations, and directing social services.

Cathy continues to share her faith, teaching others how to live life filled with God's love, study His Word, and spend time in meaningful prayer. Relaxation and refreshing for Cathy are expressed in journaling, crocheting, reading, playing piano, travelling, and cruising. Since retirement, Cathy has also been enjoying her role as a doTerra Wellness Advocate.

Ken and Cathy reside in Oshawa, Ontario, where family times and five grandchildren bring them great joy.

www.facebook.com/catherine.ritson.5

Matt Tapley has been the Lead Pastor of Lakemount Worship Centre in Grimsby, Ontario since 2008. He is a gifted leader who serves the Church by developing leaders dependent on the Spirit with full devotion to the Word of God. He frequently travels the nation as an insightful preacher, anointed worship leader, and a keen contributor to leadership team environments.

Matt and his wife, Lisa, have been happily married since August 1994. Together they have three amazing kids—Abigail ('98), Joey ('99), and Sarah ('01). In November of 2012, their youngest daughter, Sarah, died after a three-year battle with cancer. Matt's personal life message demonstrates a confident faith in declaring the relentless goodness of God no matter life's circumstances. He and Lisa continue to use their testimony to encourage others who are facing challenges of faith.

Matt is a delusional Leafs fan and also enjoys riding his Harley whenever and wherever he can.

www.lakemount.ca

Ken Vandevrie grew up in Lynden, Ontario, while Amie's childhood home was near Simcoe, Ontario. They met in 1989 while Ken was recording Amie's music in his studio. Music brought them together, and a friendship led to a beautiful love. They married in 1993 and lived in Brantford for the first thirteen years of marriage, running their business, ADS Media, together. Their next move was to Hamilton in 2006, where they have remained—running their studio and enjoying their home all in one location. Their three sons—Kurtis, Quenton, and Russel—are now pursuing their own music careers and are keen participants in assisting clients through the family business. During most weeks you'll find a Vandevrie family member joyfully serving at their home church in media, worship, or prayer. Their joy is to come alongside, encourage, and raise up other ministries and talent to build the Kingdom of God.

www.adsmedia.ca

Carl and Heide Villeseche are a young at heart couple with a real zest for life. They met in Manitoba at a Bible college, got married, and settled in St. Catharines to raise their children. Carl has enjoyed a successful career as an air traffic control supervisor for twenty-five years. While Heide's main efforts involved raising the children, she would regularly include work with pregnant teens at Hannah House in Niagara and disabled adults in Hamilton. They've always had a passion for helping family and friends, seeing people restored and inspired to reach higher, and to that end have always been active in various areas in their local church. While neither will brag about it, both are well-known for their culinary skills. Currently loving long country walks, travelling, or playing with their three grandkids, they look forward to what adventures await them in the future. They presently serve their home church in the areas of life groups and prayer ministry.

About the Author

Ruth Teakle lives with her husband, Carl, in Beamsville, Ontario. She loves to spend time with her three children and their spouses and her eleven grandchildren. Although retired, Ruth serves as a support staff member at Lakemount Worship Centre in Grimsby, Ontario, where she previously served on full-time and part-time staff for eighteen years. Her roles varied from overseeing small groups and missions to prayer and pastoral care. As well, she has led and assisted with numerous short-term missions to the Caribbean, Eastern Europe, Ukraine, South America, northern Ontario, and Quebec.

On the home front, Ruth and Carl have fostered over 130 children during a twenty-five-year period. Ruth has worked within the Correctional Services of Canada, volunteered with numerous summer camp programs through both Girls Guides of Canada and the Salvation Army, directed an annual city-wide Christmas toy program, and filmed a national training course for telephone prayer partners. She also served for many years in local, area, and national capacities with Aglow International Canada prior to pastoral ministry.

Ruth's academic pursuits have included studies at Lakeshore Teachers' College, Brock University (Bachelor of Arts), and Wagner University (Master of Practical Ministries). She has completed ESL studies, is a Certified Anger Management Specialist and Trauma Healing Facilitator. Prior to taking additional Religious Studies courses with Global University in preparation for ordained ministry, Ruth enjoyed a successful thirty-two-year career as an elementary school teacher.

Ruth's heart is to see people become passionate followers of Christ. She has a strong sense of mission to help people build healthy connections with God and others. Her challenging but victorious personal journey makes her well qualified to share on the importance of faith in our personal journeys.

Additional Note: Ruth's first devotional, *Changing Seasons*, is a pocket/purse sized devotional full of encouragement from God's Word written especially for seniors, and it's one of the GODQUEST SERIES available only through The Bible League, Canada. bibleleague.ca/resources/godquest/.

Pursuing Patience, Pursuing Peace, Choosing Love, and *Choosing Kindness* are available through Word Alive Press and numerous national and international outlets.

Ruth has also authored a delightfully illustrated children's book for children ages four to nine, *Joshua Wonders: What Does the Tooth Fairy Do with My Teeth?* available through numerous national and international outlets.

Confident
Desperate
Daring